JOHN H. MINAN

THE LITTLE
GREEN BOOK
of
GOLF LAW

The Real Rules of the Game of Golf

Foreword by Gary McCord
CBS Sports Analyst, Champions Tour Player,
and author of *Golf For Dummies*

Cover design by ABA Publishing.

The materials contained herein represent the opinions and views of the authors and/or the editors, and should not be construed to be the views or opinions of the law firms or companies that such persons are in partnership with, associated with, or employed by, or of the American Bar Association unless adopted pursuant to the bylaws of the Association.

Nothing contained in this book is to be considered as the rendering of legal advice, either generally or in connection with any specific issue or case; nor do these materials purport to explain or interpret any specific bond or policy, or any provisions thereof, issued by any particular franchise company, or to render franchise or other professional advice. Readers are responsible for obtaining advice from their own lawyers or other professionals. This book and any forms and agreements herein are intended for educational and informational purposes only.

Library of Congress Cataloging-in-Publication Data

Minan, John H.
   The little green book of golf law : the real rules of the game of golf / by John H. Minan.
      p. cm.
   Includes index.
   1. Golf–Law and legislation–United States–Cases. 2. Golf–Law and legislation–United States. I. Title

   KF3989.A7M56 2007
   344.73'099–dc22

                                  2007029152

ISBN: 978-1-59031-845-4

Discounts are available for books ordered in bulk. Special consideration is given to state bars, CLE programs, and other bar-related organizations. Inquire at Book Publishing, ABA Publishing, American Bar Association, 321 North Clark Street, Chicago, Illinois 60610-4714.

www.ababooks.org

Dedication

This book is dedicated to my son and golfing buddy, John Jr.

Table of Contents

Foreword

Golf, like every other aspect of life, is often subject to the vagaries of law. The game itself was banned by James II of Scotland in the Middle Ages (he thought it distracted the troops from practicing archery); and, since then, golf has been the subject to a whole range of litigation: from whacking your fellow golfer with a golf ball to crashing a golf cart.

Fortunately, most golfers, including myself, keep the law at arm's length on the course, even if the golfer is also a lawyer. But as Professor Jack Minan's *The Little Green Book of Golf Law* demonstrates, law permeates this game in odd ways, such as the golfer who—in a fit of rage after a bad round—attacked a bird that was also an endangered species. (A lesson to any golfer not to take his or her frustrations out on any animal on the golf course.)

As you read the following cases described in this book, I think that you will be struck—and amused—at how legal issues can arise from this game. Equally important, though, is how legal issues and conflicts are addressed and solved by the legal system. No matter where you stand on a particular issue, it's inspiring how our justice system, whether dealing with the Americans with Disabilities Act or a patent law issue, provide all individuals with their "day in court."

I hope you enjoy this book and the legal lessons it offers.

Gary McCord

Preface

The Little Green Book of Golf Law—The Real Rules of the Game of Golf deals with golf and the law. It is written for a general audience with an interest in either of these subjects. The collection of nineteen cases track the 18 holes typically played in a "stipulated round" of golf plus one for the traditional 19th "clubhouse" hole.[1]

The book contains a broad tapestry of interesting legal fireworks involving some aspect of golf. The law is a fascinating subject for people because it is both everywhere one looks and sometimes outrageous. One does not have to be a lawyer or have legal training to enjoy considering whether the cases are examples of the legal system run amok or fair judgments to be applauded. To my knowledge, no similar book on golf law exists—so it is one of a kind.

The chapters explore different sets of facts and legal issues. Each chapter heading identifies the official citation to the case for those who might like to find out more about it. Because each case is based on a different set of facts, the chapters are like short stories. As a result, they may be read in any order without diminishing the reader's enjoyment.

There are cases involving Tiger Woods' right of publicity, personal injuries occurring on-and-off the golf course, patent and trademark disagreements, a contract dispute involving a hole-in-one contest, a product liability case for a defective golf club, a criminal prosecution under the endangered species act, a fight with the Internal Revenue Service (IRS) over tax deductions for golf-related expenses, and more. The final chapter will be especially interesting to anyone who has hoisted a drink or two after finishing a round of golf.

---

1. A "stipulated round" consists of playing the holes on a golf course in their correct sequence unless otherwise authorized by the Committee. The number of holes in such a round is eighteen.

Each chapter focuses on selected issues that were litigated. In order to capture core ideas, the discussion has been simplified to minimize complexity. For example, the official case involving Tiger Woods' right of publicity is more than forty pages of single-spaced text. In the book, it is only several pages in length. Consequently, the chapters necessarily lack some of the legal detail revealed by reading the official version of the case.

At the end of each chapter, there is a section called "Inside the Rules" that explores certain aspects of the Rules of Golf ("Rules"),[2] which is the official code governing how the game is played. The United States Golf Association ("U.S.G.A.") and the Royal and Ancient Golf Club of Saint Andrews ("R&A") write, interpret, and revise the Rules every four years. The next revision is scheduled for January 1, 2008. The Decisions on the Rules of Golf ("Decisions"), which are provided by the U.S.G.A. and the R&A every two years, is another authoritative source governing the game.[3] The Decisions are written in a question and answer format, and provide answers to matters not specifically addressed by the Rules.

Many of the cases indirectly raise questions about the Rules or the Decisions that are discussed in "Inside the Rules." In *Hennessey v. Pyne*, for example, the plaintiff sued the defendant because the plaintiff was injured by a golf ball that was hit "out of bounds" by the defendant. The case provides an ideal opportunity to review the "out-of-bounds" rule. Another example is *Zurla v. Hydel*, where three golfers were playing together as a group. Most people would describe the group as a "threesome." But, as the reader will discover, the rules define the term "threesome" differently than conventional usage.

---

2. The Rules of Golf (2006-2007).
3. Decisions on the Rules of Golf (2006-2007).

An official is not usually available to ensure that the Rules are followed. Consequently, the rules are treated as self-enforced mandates by most players. Others may also get in the act. Spectators, for example, often weigh in on possible rule violations during golfing events. During the 2007 Masters, a viewer telephoned the Augusta National Golf Club claiming that Jim "Bones" Mackay, who is professional golfer Phil Mickelson's caddie, violated the assistance rule by placing Mickelson's golf bag in a position to block the sun on the eighteenth tee.[4] Mickelson told his caddie to place the bag so that it aligned with the shadow cast by a spectator on his ball. Mickelson was afraid he'd be distracted if the spectator and his shadow moved during his swing. By shadowing the ball with the bag, Michelson wouldn't notice any movement should the spectator move while he was hitting his tee shot. After reviewing a tape of the telecast, the chairman of the competition ruled that no violation had occurred.[5]

In most instances, a significant difference exists between violating the law and not playing the game according to the rules. Violating the law is apt to have far more serious consequences. The section "Inside the Rules," which follows each case, is designed to highlight certain aspects of how the game should be played. The Decisions are more than five hundred pages in length, whereas the "Inside the Rules" discussion is only a paragraph or two. Thus, the discussion is intended to be illustrative rather than comprehensive.

---

4. Rule 14-2 states that "a player must not accept physical assistance or protection from the elements."

5. Tod Leonard, "*Mickelson survives TV replay review*," San Diego Union Tribune, Apr. 3, 2007, at C4. If Mickelson had been found to have violated Rule 14-2, he would be subject to a two-stroke penalty and disqualification for signing an incorrect score card were the violation not reported.

The book is not a substitute for legal advice. The law is dynamic. Its application is affected by the facts as well as applicable statutes and judicial rulings. The law also may vary among states. Finally, lawyers frequently disagree as to what a particular case actually held or means. These considerations suggest that actual legal problems involving golf should be referred to a lawyer.

For the love of the game

P.J. O'Rourke may have captured the elementary nature of the game when he said that it combines two favorite pastimes: taking long walks and hitting things with a stick. But the love of the game was more aptly revealed in the 1996 film classic *Tin Cup*. Roy "Tin Cup" McAvoy (played by Kevin Costner) and Dr. Molly Griswold (played by Rene Russo) exchange their views on the game:

Molly: *"This is, without a doubt, the stupidest, silliest, most idiotic grotesquery masquerading as a game that has ever been invented."*

Tin Cup (cheerfully responding): *"Yes ma'am, that's why I love it."*

The Little Green Book of Golf Law allows me the joy of sharing my passion for golf as well as the law.

I am indebted to my colleagues at the University of San Diego School of Law who have aided me with their comments, guidance, and support. I extend special thanks to Dean Kevin Cole, Nancy Carter, Adam Kolber, William Lawrence, David McGowan, Frank Partnoy, Mike Reed, and Dick Speidel. I also extend a special thanks to Lindsay O'Hair, my research assistant at USD and member of the San Diego Law Review, for her diligence and thoroughness. Finally, I wish to thank Jeff Ninnemann of the Southern California Golf Association for his review and comments on the materials in "Inside the Rules."

I welcome your comments and suggestions for changes or other cases to be included in future updates. Enjoy the following stories of legal intrigue.

John H. Minan
Professor of Law
University of San Diego School of Law
San Diego, CA 92110

Introduction

For those who find it useful, this Introduction provides a short overview of the American courts and system for reporting judicial decisions. The federal court system consists of trial courts (U.S. District Courts, the U.S. Tax Court, and the U.S. Court of Federal Claims), courts of appeal, and the U.S. Supreme Court. In addition, each state has its own court system based on its state constitution or authorizing legislation. State courts generally decide cases dealing with state law, while federal courts decide cases arising under federal law. Congress has given the federal courts exclusive authority over certain types of cases, such as patent, trademark, and federal tax issues.

Understanding the hierarchy of the court system is important to understanding the significance of a decision. A trial court is the lowest court in the hierarchy. It may be thought of as the base of the judicial pyramid. The trial court usually is the starting point for the litigants. It is responsible for deciding the case by determining the facts, often with the aid of a jury, and then applying the law to those facts.

A litigant dissatisfied with the result in the trial court may appeal. Two levels of appellate courts exist in the federal system and in most states. Intermediate appellate courts are one level above the trial courts. The court of last resort or highest level of appeal is at the apex of the judicial pyramid. It has the final say on the matter appealed to it.

In a state system, the court of last resort is usually called the Supreme Court. This name is not always used to describe the highest court, however. In New York and Maryland, for example, the court of last resort is called the Court of Appeals. Regardless of its official title, the state court of final resort is the highest judicial authority on all matters of state law, and its decisions are binding on all lower courts within the state. The title given to the intermediate appellate courts also varies by state, although the most common title is court of appeals. Intermediate appellate courts may be organized by geographical districts, such as in California, or by subject matter. As a practical matter, intermediate appellate courts handle most of the appeals within their state.

In the federal system, the court of last resort is the United States Supreme Court. It is the final judicial authority on all questions of federal law, and has the power to review and decide any decision of a state court regarding the application of federal law. Federal Courts of Appeals are organized geographically by circuits, and typically review district court decisions in their respective circuits. There are eleven federal circuits, a District of Columbia Circuit, and a Federal Circuit.

The function of appellate courts is to decide whether the law was correctly applied. With a few exceptions, factual determinations made by the trial court are not disturbed on appeal. When the trial court makes an error of law, the intermediate court of appeal exists to correct it. If the error is not corrected, the dissatisfied litigant may then ask the court of final resort to set the matter right. An incorrect decision will be reversed and often sent back (remanded) by the reviewing appellate court to the lower court so that the law can be correctly applied. If the law was correctly applied, the reviewing court will affirm the decision.

Appellate courts often write opinions explaining their decisions. Under the doctrine of precedent, these written opinions are binding on lower courts in the judicial pyramid. These opinions are published in bound volumes, known as reporters, which are available to the legal community and the public. Most states have their own reporters for publishing opinions. In addition, regional reporters collect and publish state decisions on a broad geographical basis.

State regional reporters and state reporters were used to locate many of the cases in this book. For those who might want to read a decision in its entirety, the official citation is given in the heading of each chapter and can be found on various electronic databases such as Lexis and Westlaw. *Hennessey v. Pyne*, can be found in Volume 694 of the Atlantic (Second Series) regional reporter at page 691. *Morgan v. Fuji Country U.S.A., Inc.* can be found in the California state reporter, Volume 34 of the Fourth California Appellate Series at page 127. In addition to state court decisions, certain administrative decisions have the force of law. The *City of Santa Barbara* decision (Chapter Eighteen) of the State Water Resources Control Board illustrates this type of decision.

The federal reporter system can be used to locate federal cases. The Federal Supplement Reporter contains U.S. district court trial opinions. Cases from the intermediate Federal Courts of Appeals, also called U.S. circuit courts, are printed in the Federal Reporter Series. *ETW Corp. v. Jireh Publishing, Inc.*, may be found in volume 332 of the Federal Reporter, Third Series, at page 915. The reference "(6th Cir. 2003)" indicates that the opinion was written by the U.S. Court of Appeals for the Sixth Circuit in 2003. The *Wilson Sporting Goods v. David Geoffrey & Associates* may be located in Volume 904 of the Federal Reporter, Second Series, at page 677.

If an opinion is not written or published in a reporter, the complaint, answer, motions, and other filings may be found, although it's more difficult. These documents are part of the public record. Two cases in the book come from such publicly available documents: *State v. Terry Pupus* and *Kurash v. J.C. Resorts, Inc.*

Hole One

Hawaii:

State v. Terry Pupus, LNR T1, LNR T2 (Hawaii 1997)

Bad Day of Golf Results in Criminal Prosecution

The state bird of Hawaii, however unlikely, is a goose. More specifically, it is the Nene, known to bird lovers as *Nesochen sandwicensis* or *Bernicata sandwicensis*.[6] This species is the lone survivor of a community of grazing waterfowl that inhabited the Hawaiian Islands long before the coming of the Polynesians. Scientists speculate that the Nene was once nearly identical to the Canada goose, but after thousands of years of evolution, they are now quite distinct. Because the Nene's wings are relatively weak, they do not fly as much as other geese.

The Nene is an endangered species, and protected from harm by both state and federal law.[7] Approximately 800 to 1000 Nene geese live in the wild throughout the Hawaiian Islands, with about 250 of the birds inhabiting the island of Maui.

The Sandalwood Golf Course, which opened to the public in 1991, is located in the Waikapu Valley on Maui. It is set into the West Maui mountain range and has a commanding view of

---

6. Haw. Rev. Stat. § 5-17 (1997) designates it the state bird.
7. The trumpeting sound of the Nene goose may be heard at http://www.thewild ones.org/Animals/nene.html.

the Pacific Ocean. From the blue tees, the course is somewhat over 6400 yards. In addition to being a challenging golf course, it is also home to a small group of wild Nene. The game of golf can bring out the best in a person, or the worst. In Terry Pupus's case it was the worst. Terry presumably was having a particularly bad day of golf in July of 1997. After teeing off on the par four, sixteenth hole, he encountered three Nene grazing near the teeing ground.[8] In a fit of rage, undoubtedly triggered by a bad round or irked by the mischievous Menehunes trolling the golf course, he attacked the birds.[9] Using his driver, a Callaway Big Bertha, he clubbed to death one of the three birds, a four-month-old male. The dead Nene was two to three pounds and stood a foot high. According to official records, the bird was born in early 1997 and raised at the Maui Bird Conservation Center before being released into the wild and settling in the Sandalwood area.

Pupus struck the bird with blows described by a golfer paired with the goose slayer as "Jose Canseco-style swings." In

8. The term "tee box" is commonly used by players to describe the place where they make their tee shot. The proper name is the "teeing ground."
9. Menehune are the legendary mischievous "little people" of Hawaii who are similar to pixies or trolls.

the onslaught described by the witness, the bird suffered eight fractures, its wing was fractured in several places, and its neck was broken. Immediately after killing the bird, Pupus drove off in his golf cart to resume play, unaware that he would have an up-coming date with the law.

Pupus was prosecuted by the state on charges of cruelty to animals and for violating the state indigenous wildlife act.[10] Although Terry claimed he "accidentally" hit the bird, eyewitness testimony contradicted his questionable version of the facts. Terry was found guilty as charged, fined $4000, ordered to perform 300 hours of community service, and placed on a year's probation. Not surprisingly, the court said that it had no sympathy whatsoever for Mr. Pupus.

In surely what was a surprise to this frustrated golfer, the prosecuting attorney also argued Pupus should forfeit *all* his golf clubs. Big Bertha's criminal associates, if you will.

The law of forfeiture has a long pedigree in both English and American law.[11] The central idea of the law is that the property itself has committed the crime and should be relinquished to the state.

Hawaii law authorizes the forfeiture of an item used in the commission of a crime. The court rejected full forfeiture of all his clubs as being unduly punitive, ordering instead that only the weapon used in the attack be seized and forfeited. Pupus got his clubs back, minus his Big Bertha, which was the weapon used to kill the bird.

---

10. Haw. Rev. Stat. § 711-1109 (1997); Hawaii Administrative Rules Section 13-124-(3). My thanks are extended to Detective Daniel J. Minan, formerly with the Criminal Investigation Section, Hawaii County Police Department, for his detective work on this caper and for providing these citations.

11. The United States Supreme Court recently reviewed the constitutional limitations to the law of forfeiture in *Bennis v. Michigan*, 516 U.S. 442 (1996). The Court held that a wife's interest in an automobile used by her spouse to commit a crime did not prevent its forfeiture.

State v. Terry Pupus reminds one of "The Rime of the Ancient Mariner" by Samuel Taylor Coleridge. The mariner, now played by Pupus, is hounded by disaster after senselessly murdering an albatross, now played by the deceased Nene. The disaster for Pupus was the public humiliation associated with being found guilty of violating the law of Hawaii. The hope is that Pupus, like the mariner, ultimately realized the gravity of his action and accepted responsibility for it.

Inside the Rules of Golf, Section I: "Etiquette"

The game of golf is intended to be enjoyable. The Rules of Golf contain etiquette guidelines to assist in making it enjoyable for all involved. Among other things, they provide that players should "conduct themselves in a disciplined manner, demonstrating courtesy and sportsmanship at all times." Clubbing wildlife, talking during another player's backswing, moving when in another player's sightline, and humming like Gene Kelly in the rain are all no-nos. A golfer should avoid distracting another player when he or she is trying to concentrate.

The foremost principle of golf etiquette is safety. Golf courses can be dangerous places. In April 2007, for example, an argument erupted over the ownership of a golf ball retrieved from a water hazard on the sixth hole of the Oceanside Municipal Golf Course in Southern California. The resulting melee landed one golfer in the hospital and Bishop Michael Babin, an Oceanside minister of the cloth, and his playing companions in court charged with felony assault.[12]

Art imitates life. In the movie *Sideways*, Miles (played by Paul Giamatti) and Jack (played by Thomas Hayden Church)

---

12. Krista Davis, "*Minister to be arraigned in assault at golf course*," San Diego Union Tribune, Apr. 3, 2007, at B3.

wrestle with life's frustrations during their week-long tour of California's wine country. During a scene where they are playing golf, Miles loses his temper after someone from the group playing behind them hits a ball near them. The situation dangerously escalates when Miles hits a ball back at them.

The Rules of Golf do not expressly cover this type of breach of etiquette. An official decision to the Rules does address, however, the *Sideways* angry-player situation: Does a player violate the rules on playing a practice stroke (Rule 7) or the wrong ball (Rule 15) when, after almost being hit by a ball from someone playing in a group behind, reacts by hitting the ball back toward that group?

The official answer is no. No explanation or detail accompanies the answer. The return volley by the angry golfer does not comfortably fit within the concept of "practice." But the situation does arguably meet the definition of the "wrong ball," which includes hitting any ball other than the player's ball, including "another player's ball."

The official decision does not, however, let the miscreant off without penalty. "In equity," the angry player incurs the general penalty of loss of hole in match play or two strokes in stroke play under Rule 1-4.[13] The result is the same as would be the case under the wrong ball or practice rule.

Slow pace of play is a source of frayed tempers. Firing into a group like "Yosemite Sam" to encourage them to speed up or as Miles did in *Sideways* is always dangerous.[14] It can have unintended consequences, including an unwanted visit with a lawyer and the legal system.

---

13. Decision 1-4/4 (2006-07).
14. "Yosemite Sam" is the irascible Looney Tunes cartoon character known for wildly shooting his six-guns whenever and wherever he had the urge.

7

Hole Two

Federal:

ETW Corp. v. Jireh Publishing, Inc.,
332 F.3d 915 (6th Cir. 2003)

"The Masters of Augusta"

Eldrick "Tiger" Woods has had an unprecedented professional career since becoming a pro golfer in the late summer of 1996. In 1997, at age twenty-one, Tiger became the youngest player to win the renowned Augusta Masters Tournament. He won the event by a convincing 12-stroke margin. By 2007, Tiger had collected four "green jackets" from his victories at the Masters, a number suitable to outfit a well-dressed foursome of leprechauns on St. Patrick's Day.

In addition to being one of the world's most recognized golfers and celebrities, Tiger is a major business enterprise. Before playing in his first tournament as a professional, Tiger signed endorsement contracts estimated at $70 million. Eldrick "Tiger" Woods, Inc. ("Woods"), Tiger's commercial merchandising arm, holds the exclusive right to manage his publicity rights, including his name, image, likeness and signature. The company also owns the U.S. trademark "Tiger Woods," which includes the right to use his name in connection with "art prints" and other memorabilia.

To what extent does the law limit the commercial use of Tiger's image and identity by others?

The legal fireworks in *ETW Corp. v. Jireh Publishing, Inc.*

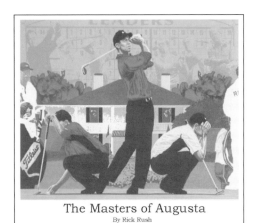

The Masters of Augusta
By Rick Rush

www.RickRushArt.com

started in 1998 following Tiger's first triumph at Augusta. Rick Rush, who bills himself as "America's sports artist," created a limited edition painting depicting the 1997 event. Striking various golfing poses, the painting captures Tiger on the prowl. Also shown in the painting are two caddies (one being Tiger's caddy at the time, "Fluff" Cowan) as well as the Augusta National Clubhouse. Hovering in the sky-blue background, presumably providing an artistic connection to the past, are the images of well-known golfing legends—Arnold Palmer, Sam Snead, Ben Hogan, Walter Hagen, Bobby Jones, and Jack Nicklaus. Rush's signature appears in the bottom right-hand corner above the title "The Masters of Augusta."

The publisher of the artwork, and target of the lawsuit, was Jireh Publishing. According to the court documents, it sold 250 serigraphs (prints made by a silkscreen process) for $700 apiece, and 5000 lithographs (prints made by an ink-impression process) for $100 a piece. The painting and prints were very similar to a poster of Woods sold by Nike under a license from Woods. Not surprisingly, there was no dispute that Wood's likeness in Rush's artwork was reproduced for commercial profit.

Woods fired a "stinger" at the defendant by suing in the Federal District Court for the Northern District of Ohio for trademark infringement, unfair competition, deceptive trade practices, and violation of his right of publicity.[15] Tiger's awesome prowess on the golf course didn't translate into a legal victory. The court dismissed the complaint. It found that the use of Tiger's trademarked name was "fair use" under established principles of trademark law, that Tiger's image in the painting was not protected under the argued theories, and that the Master's painting by Rush was protected by the First Amendment.[16]

Tiger did not lose graciously; he appealed to the Sixth Circuit Court of Appeals. On June 20, 2003, the court of appeals affirmed the district court, and six weeks later denied the request for a rehearing. The appellate court applied three related legal rules. First, it applied an *ad hoc* balancing approach, which balanced Woods' proprietary right of publicity against Rush's right to free expression. Second, it construed the right of publicity as being limited by "fair-use" principles contained in federal copyright law. Finally, it found that Rush's work satisfied the "transformativeness test" because the artwork consisted of much more than a mere literal depiction of Tiger Woods. It was a panorama of Woods' victory, with all the trappings of the tournament presented. In short, it was a portrayal of a historic sporting event that Tiger happened to win.

The right of publicity, the first legal rule applied by the court, is a relatively new type of intellectual property right. The right is a creature of state law, in this case Ohio, and its violation gives rise to a cause of action for the commercial tort of unfair competition. Under this theory, a famous person, such as Tiger Woods, has the general right to exploit his name or

---

15. A "stinger" is a specialty golf shot popularized by Tiger Woods. Instead of using a driver or 3-wood off the tee, Tiger sometimes uses a two-iron to hit a low-boring screamer that goes about 270 yards.

16. U.S. Const. amend. I. "Congress shall make no law ... abridging the freedom of speech ..."

likeness for financial gain. The Restatement (Third) of Unfair Competition, Section 46, which is followed in Ohio, generally defines the right of publicity: "One who appropriates the commercial value of a person's identity by using without consent the person's name, likeness, or other indicia of identity for purposes of trade is subject to liability."

As recognized by the court, the right to benefit from one's celebrity status has constitutional limits. In balancing the competing interests between the artist and the celebrity, the right to free expression, as guaranteed by the First Amendment, is accorded substantial weight. The court states:

> After balancing the societal and personal interests embodied in the First Amendment against Woods's property rights, we conclude that the effect of limiting Woods's right of publicity in this case is negligible and significantly outweighed by society's interest in freedom of artistic expression. In this case, we find that Woods's right of publicity must yield to the First Amendment.

Tiger is as aggressive in the courts in attempting to protect his "right to publicity" as he is in attempting to win every golf tournament. But as this case illustrates, he does not always win.

Inside the Rules, Rule 1: "The game"

The Rules of Golf ("Rules") govern the game made famous by the legendary golfers depicted in Rick Rush's painting "The Masters of Augusta." The Rules define the nature of the sport in the following way: "The game of golf consists of playing a ball from the teeing ground into the hole by a stroke or successive strokes *in accordance* with the Rules." They also state that no player "shall take any action to influence the position or movement of a ball except in accordance with the Rules." Like any set of rules, however, not every circumstance can be anticipated. Any situation not directly covered by a rule is governed "in accordance with equity." While the phrase "in accordance with equity" is necessarily elastic, and thus not defined by the Rules, the official U.S.G.A. Decisions on the Rules of Golf ("Decisions") reflect the core idea as treating similar situations similarly. In its broadest and most general sense, the phrase embodies the principle of fairness.

Although various rules will be discussed in subsequent chapters, two principles bind the rules together. One is the requirement that a golfer accept the lie of the ball as it is found on the golf course, unless a specific exception is granted to do otherwise. This principle was captured in the novel *The Gods of Golf*.[17]

> Pick a ball, any ball at all
> But never, ever let it fall ...
> For if it falls, and fall it may
> You must play it where it lays!

The second principle is that a golfer must play the same ball on each hole without handling it until the hole is finished unless the Rules permit a substitution. There are only a few exceptions. Some exceptions are if the ball is unfit for play (Rule 5-3), in a water hazard (Rule 26), lost or out of bounds (Rule 27), or unplayable (Rule 28), a player may substitute another ball. A player may change balls after finishing one hole and starting the next one.

---

17. David L. Smith and John P Holms, The Gods of Golf, 115 (1996).

Hole Three

Rhode Island:

Hennessey v. Pyne,
694 A.2d 691 (R.I. 1997)

Out-of-bounds on the left:

Golf Course Liability to Neighbor for Personal Injury

After returning home from church on a pleasant Sunday morning in mid-September, Eileen Hennessey stopped to smell the flowers in her front-yard garden. Her morning reverie amidst the summer flora was abruptly interrupted when she was hit in the head by a golf ball. Sometimes it can be dangerous to stop and smell the flowers.

Eileen Hennessey lived next to the Rhode Island Louisquisset Golf Club. Her condominium was located on the crook of the dogleg on the eleventh hole. From the teeing ground, the hole swerved slightly to the left. Her back yard was about fourteen feet from the edge of the out-of-bounds marker and approximately halfway down the fairway from the teeing ground.

Eileen testified that she did not see the ball coming because trees blocked her view of the eleventh-hole teeing area. The golf course's assistant pro, Michael Pyne, hit the wayward shot, which was modestly described in court documents as having "veered slightly left." He airmailed the shot; the problem was it had the wrong address.

This was not the first time Eileen had trouble with golfers. Players regularly peppered her condominium with golf balls.

She testified at her deposition that for approximately five years, during the heaviest part of the playing season, her condominium was hit "about ten times a day." Eileen claimed that sometimes her condominium was hit twice in the same day by the same golfer. Presumably, these repeat offenders were simply following the Rules of Golf on out-of-bounds or lost balls.

She was not alone in her knowledge of the problem. Michael Pyne, the assistant pro and author of the misfired shot, knew about the location of the condominiums and of the propensity for the club's golfers to strafe them with misfired golf shots.

Eileen tried to protect herself and her property from damage caused by errant golf balls. She installed Plexiglas in various windows of her home because of the frequency with which golf balls pelted the exterior and broke her glass windows.

Eileen Hennessey sued Michael Pyne on a variety of theories, including assault and battery. The Supreme Court of Rhode Island said the trial court was correct in dismissing her claim of assault and battery. It also rejected her nuisance claim and her husband's loss-of-consortium claim. But Michael was not out of the woods, where in truth he would have been better off. The supreme court concluded that the trial court should not have dismissed her claim of negligence and that she should be given the opportunity to prove negligence. The matter was sent back to the trial court for consideration of her negligence claim against Michael because the record was incomplete on this issue.[18] Although I do not know how Eileen fared

---

18. The record does not indicate certain other facts that might materially affect her negligence claim. These include: How many yards the golf hole was from the tee? How many strokes were par for the hole? What golf club was used by Pyne on the tee? What was the exact distance of Hennessey's front-yard garden and condominium from the tee? It is also unclear from the record whether Pyne actually saw, or could have seen, Eileen from where he addressed the ball on the tee. Finally, the record does not indicate whether Pyne shouted "fore" or attempted to give any warning either before or after he saw his tee shot heading off the course and toward Hennessey's condominium.

on remand, I am reasonably confident that she never took golf lessons from Michael.

The Law of Assault and Battery

Although various theories of liability were argued, her assault and battery claims are most interesting. Why did the Supreme Court reject Eileen's claim of assault and battery? In short, the facts did not match her legal theories.

Claims of assault and battery may be prosecuted by the state as crimes, or by private parties as torts. Broadly speaking, a tort is a civil wrong, other than a breach of contract, which a court will remedy by awarding damages. Eileen sued in tort because she wanted money. Assault and battery are two different types of intentional torts. It is common to speak of assault and battery in one breath because the facts that give rise to the claims often support the applicability of both theories. Nevertheless, they are separate legal theories that require a plaintiff to prove different elements in order to prevail.

The law of assault protects a person from the apprehension or fear of harmful or offensive contact. The defendant must intend that the plaintiff apprehend or fear the contact. In addition, the defendant's act must create a reasonable apprehension of immediate harmful or offensive contact to the plaintiff because the law does not protect against exaggerated fears of contact.

In order for the plaintiff to be in reasonable apprehension, he or she must obviously be aware of the defendant's threatening act. Eileen was not aware of Michael's presence on the teeing ground; much less did she fear any injury from the errant golf ball that ultimately hit her. Thus, she was unable to establish the critical fact that she had any reasonable apprehension of imminent bodily harm from Michael's conduct. In addition, Eileen failed to prove that Michael had the necessary intent needed to establish a compensable claim under the law of assault.

In contrast to assault, battery is harmful or offensive contact with the plaintiff's person that is caused by an act of the defendant who intended to produce such a result. The law of battery protects individuals from intentional and unpermitted contacts. It protects a person's body, as well as anything closely associated with the person so as to be identified with the individual's personal dignity, such as his or her clothing. In the words of the court, a battery is "an act that was intended to cause, and in fact did cause, 'an offensive contact with or unconsented touching of or trauma upon the body of another, thereby generally resulting in the consummation of the assault … Intent to injure plaintiff, however, is unnecessary in a situation in which a defendant willfully sets in motion a force that in its ordinary course causes the injury.'"

Eileen argued that Michael intentionally hit the golf ball that in turn struck her and thus his act was a battery. Her reasoning was not persuasive to the court. There was no evidence that he intended to hit her with the wayward ball.

Michael's intent was limited to committing a "battery" on the ball, and perhaps on the fairway by taking a divot, followed by a "battery" to the green when his ball landed, followed by a possible one-putt "battery" on the hole. But his intent was limited to these types of batteries.

While it was indisputable that Michael's teeing off on the ball willfully set in motion a force, namely hitting the ball, that force did not "in its ordinary course" cause Eileen's injury. Indeed, if the ball had traveled "in its ordinary course," at least after having been hammered by the golf club's assistant pro, we can safely assume that it would have headed for the fairway rather than for Eileen Hennessey's head.

Inside the Rules, Rule 27: "Out of bounds"

The phrase "out of bounds" (OB) is important under the Rules as well as legally. The phrase is used to describe the area beyond the boundaries of the course or any part of the course marked as out of bounds. In *Hennessy v. Pyne*, Eileen Hennessy was injured by a golf ball hit by Michael Pyne. Because Eileen was in her front yard when she was hit, there is no doubt that the golf ball was "beyond the boundaries of the course." The rules prohibit a golfer from playing a ball that lies out of bounds. Rule 27 would require Michael to play another ball from the spot (or as nearly as possible to that spot) from which he hit the out-of-bounds ball that clobbered Eileen. He also would be subject to two separate penalties under the Rules. First, a one-stroke penalty would be added to his score for hitting his ball out of bounds. Second, he would have to go back to the original spot to hit another shot (stroke) and be penalized "loss of distance."

Hole Four

Illinois:

Zurla v. Hydel,
681 N.E.2d 148 (Ill. 1997)

Liability to a Golfer in the Same "Foursome"

I n golf, a golf ball hit by a right-handed player that curves to the left is called a hook. One that curves to the right is called a slice. If it goes straight, some call it a miracle. This case is about an untimely miracle.

Gerald Zurla, Victor Hydel, and Edward Vrdolyak were golfing buddies from Chicago, Illinois. They decided to head to Florida for a relaxing weekend of golf, fishing, and probably a few beers.

Gerald and Edward were the experienced golfers in the threesome, whereas Victor was the novice. They had played one uneventful round of golf at the Lely Resort in Naples, Florida, prior to their second and fateful round on the links. One can only hope that their fishing was less eventful than their golf.

Things turned sour on the fourth hole, a straightaway par four. Victor, the novice, sliced his tee shot about 100 to 130 yards on the right side of the fairway. Gerald and Edward fared better. Their shots landed approximately 225 yards from the tee box in the general direction of the green. After teeing off, the threesome drove their carts to Victor's ball. Victor was told to take the club he needed and wait until they returned from finding their shots before hitting his second shot. Gerald and Edward then went off to find their tee shots. They found their balls and parked the carts next to them.

In the meantime, a slow-moving foursome was on the green ahead of them. Victor saw the group leave the green. As Gerald watched the foursome move on to the fifth tee box, he walked up to the ridge of a sand bunker to get a better view of the fourth green.

Thinking his playing partners were safely positioned away from the green, Victor, eager to get on with the round, launched his second shot. He was wrong. Unlike his tee shot, Victor's next effort flew straight and true. Unfortunately for Gerald, who had turned his back to the green and had begun walking back to his cart, Victor's ball struck him in the head, causing injury.

No longer the buddies they once were, Gerald sued Victor alleging that Victor had negligently hit the golf ball that whacked him. His theory of liability included the argument that the proper standard of care should be the same as in any ordinary negligence case, namely Victor owed the duty to exercise reasonable and ordinary care for the safety of others.

Victor responded that an allegation of simple negligence was insufficient under Illinois law to allow Gerald to recover damages.[19] Victor's theory was that, in a sporting event, no liability exists for injuries caused by negligent conduct between participants because injury is foreseeable and not uncommon. Liability, he said, attaches only for intentional or reckless conduct, a higher level of wrongdoing. More specifically, he argued that participants in "contact sports" owe a duty to refrain only

---

19. Personal injury suits between Illinois residents are governed by Illinois law even though the injury occurred in another state.

from willful and wanton conduct, and that his conduct did not breach this legal standard.

The trial court rejected Victor's legal argument, but certified the legal question of the relevant standard to use in such cases to the appellate court because a higher-level Illinois court had not yet resolved the relevant standard of care between golfers.

The Relevant Standard of Care: Willful and Wanton Conduct or Negligence?

Gary M. Crist, the general counsel for the National Golf Foundation, stated in *Golf Digest* magazine that the misfiring golfer is rarely held responsible for his or her errant shot.[20] He observed that unless the wayward shot was hit purposely or maliciously, liability is not likely. Essentially, this was Victor's theory—he had not acted in a willful or wanton manner, and therefore, should not be found liable.

In contrast to this standard, the law of negligence generally requires a person to exercise a reasonable degree of safety toward those who are within the zone of danger of that person's activities. In other words, an individual is under a legal duty to act as a prudent and reasonable person. If an injury is traceable to the breach of this duty of care, the person causing the injury may be held liable for the negligence absent the availability of some affirmative defense, such as the injured person assuming the risk of injury.

The standard of ordinary care found in the law of negligence has not been uniformly applied to participants in various types of sporting events. In some sports, physical contact or the risk of injury is an inherent part of the game. Some states

---

20. Gary M. Crist, *Golf Digest*, Apr. 1998, at 38.

23

have applied a different standard of care to participants playing contact sports[21] or active sports.[22] In those jurisdictions, liability results only if the conduct causing the injury is intentional or reckless. Ordinary negligence is excused on the theory that the players are aware both of the inherent risks of the game and possible injury. This awareness, combined with the nature of the sport, may lead competitors to be more physically aggressive and less careful than they otherwise would be.

The appellate court rejected this approach to liability. It reasoned:

> [G]olf is simply not the type of game in which participants are inherently, inevitably or customarily struck by the ball. Unlike the contact sports recognized by the cases, the only defense of the target in golf is made by the principles of Sir Issac Newton, the natural obstacles of Mother Nature and the cunning of those who

---

21. In *Thompson v. McNeill*, 53 Ohio St.3d 102, 559 N.E.2d 705 (Ohio 1990), the Ohio Supreme Court opined that injury to a golfer during a golf game was foreseeable and not uncommon. It followed the traditional standard of not holding a golfer liable for an injury sustained by another golfer unless the golfer acted intentionally or recklessly. In reaching this conclusion, the court rejected the distinction between contact and non-contact sports. "The contact-non-contact distinction does not sufficiently take into account that we are dealing with a spectrum of duties and risks rather than an "either-or" distinction. Is golf a contact sport? Obviously, a golfer accepts the risk of coming in contact with wayward golf shots on the links, so golf is more dangerous than table tennis, for instance, but certainly not as dangerous as kickboxing." Although the contact-non-contact distinction was rejected by the Ohio Supreme Court, it held that an injured person may only recover for injuries from an errant golf ball when the conduct of the golfer hitting the ball was intentional or reckless.

22. *Dilger v. Moyles*, 54 Cal. App. 4th 1452 (1997). Plaintiff argued that defendant, who injured plaintiff by hitting an errant shot, was negligent in failing to yell the warning of "fore." The appellate court reasoned that golf etiquette requires a player whose shot may endanger another to warn him or her by shouting "fore," but this etiquette does not impose a legal duty to shout "fore." If no legal duty was owed, the defense of primary assumption of the risk completely bars recovery. The court held that such a failure to yell "fore" was not intentional or reckless conduct outside the range of ordinary activity and was within the inherent risk of the game.

have designed the course. There is never a need for players to touch one another. Rather, golf is a sport which is contemplative and careful, with emphasis placed on control and finesse, rather than speed or raw strength. Although the game of golf certainly presents significant dangers, these dangers are more psychological than physical. Moreover, the physical dangers that exist are diminished by long-standing traditions in which courtesy between the players prevails. In such an environment, players have the time to consider the consequences of their actions and to guard against injury to those who may be in harms way.

The court said that ordinary principles of negligence apply. Therefore, Gerald need only allege and prove ordinary negligence to recover damages, not willful and wanton conduct on Victor's part.

The case was sent back to the trial court to determine whether Victor was negligent in hitting the ball when he did, rather than waiting. On remand to the trial court, a jury might find Victor negligent because he, in the exercise of reasonable care, should have known that Gerald was in the line of the intended flight of the ball, or close to it, so that the danger of hitting him should have been anticipated. By hitting, Victor increased the risk of harm to his playing partners. Moreover, Victor failed to give an audible warning of his intention to hit again or when the ball was in the air by yelling "fore." His legal defense also is weakened by the fact that he was told by his companions to wait before hitting until they had returned from finding their shots. Under the circumstances, the fact that Victor was a novice golfer did not help him.

Inside the Rules, Rule 29: "Threesomes and foursomes"

Definitions are important to correctly applying any rule. Golfers conventionally use the term "threesome" to describe three people playing golf together. In *Zurla v. Hydel*, most golfers would describe Gerald, Victor and Edward as playing together as a "threesome." But the term "threesome" has a special meaning in the Rules, and one that is not obvious. The term refers to an unusual form of play where one person plays against two other players who play alternate strokes with the same ball. Think of it as one side against the other side.

Golfers conventionally refer to four golfers playing together as a foursome. But Rules define the term foursome as "a match in which two play against two, and each side plays one ball." This type of competition is used in the Ryder Cup. The term "matches," found in the definitions section to the Rules, defines these and other types of matches.

Hole Five

New Jersey:

Maussner v. Atlantic City Country Club, Inc., 691 A.2d 826 (N.J. 1997)

A Golfer's Prayer

addyshack I is a film classic.[23] In the film, Bishop Bickering, played by Henry Wilcoxon, is depicted as fervently hoping to finish his round of golf at Bushwood Country Club. After sinking an unbelievable putt in the middle of a torrential thunder and lightning storm, he asks his caddie Carl Spackler, played by the comedian Bill Murray, "Well, what do you think?" Carl says, "I'd keep playing, I don't think the heavy stuff is going to come down for quite a while." The Bishop confidently replies, "You're right. Anyway, the good Lord would never disrupt the best game of my life. I'm infallible, young fella." The Bishop is then hit by lightning.

Life often imitates art, so the saying goes. Neither wind nor rain could keep one group of New Jersey golfers from their appointed Sunday morning round of golf at the Atlantic City Country Club. Spencer Van Maussner, Michael McHugh, Robert Dusz, and Peter Costanzo optimistically teed off, notwithstanding the fact that the sky was overcast with misty conditions and drizzling rain. At about eight o'clock, the Club's starter directed

---

23. The dialog is available at http://www.script-o-rama.com/movie_scripts/c/caddy shack-script-transcript-golf-movie.html

29

the foursome to start their round on the tenth hole. After playing the tenth and eleventh holes, the drizzle turned into a downpour.

The downpour subsided when they teed off on the twelfth hole. After hitting his approach shot to the twelfth green, Michael McHugh saw a lightning bolt. An ominous message was sent and received. The four players, accompanied by their two caddies, set off along the fairway intending to seek refuge at the clubhouse, which was about a half-mile away. No manmade shelters stood between the group and the clubhouse. Apparently being unfamiliar with Ben Franklin's experiment with lightning, Spencer put up his umbrella to protect himself from the rain.

The group crossed onto the seventh fairway on the way to the clubhouse. Suddenly there was a tremendous clap of thunder and a bolt of lightning hit Spencer. One golfer immediately went for help at the clubhouse, which was then some 325 yards away, while another golfer remained behind to assist by administering CPR to Spencer until the police and the medics arrived. According to Michael McHugh, the club caddie master and club pro arrived on the scene about the same time as the police.

Lightning continued to streak across the sky, but no one else was struck. As you might anticipate, Spencer sustained significant injuries.

Spencer sued the Country Club and the shareholders of the club alleging negligence. The defendants moved to dismiss the complaint on the theory that they had no duty to protect Spencer from a lightning strike—his injuries were the result of an act of God. The trial court judge ruled for the defendants. In his decision granting summary judgment, the judge stated:

> I don't find, in any of the case law, any duty on the part of a country club to protect against acts of God. The storm, or the lightning portion of the storm, at least, appears to have been unanticipated. Whether it was or not, when the first bolt of lightning struck, it was equally visible to [plaintiff] as it was to the pro or assistant pro … back in the shop, and he chose to expose himself by walking across the open fairways heading back to the pro shop.

The trial judge also suggested that Spencer should have taken refuge in the houses along the fairways or in a grove of trees or got down as close to the ground as possible putting himself in a fetal position if he was concerned about being struck by lightning. The judge reasoned that he did not "see that anything that the country club did, even if it might be considered negligent or less than the optimum … caused this injury to the plaintiff." He held that "the proximate cause was, first of all, an act of God, the lightning, and secondly, the injured golfer's own activities in exposing himself to the possibility of being struck by lightning." In short, the trial judge found that the country club could not be held liable for injuries resulting from God's handiwork.

Spencer appealed the trial judge's decision, and the Superior Court of New Jersey, Appellate Division, reversed. Spencer argued that the evidence raised material issues of fact that made deciding the case as a "matter of law" inappropriate. In short, the jury should decide whether the Club was somehow negligent in failing to exercise reasonable care under the circumstances.

Acts of God and Golf

Most golfers are intimately familiar with acts of God. This seems clear from the fact that many golfers regularly invoke His name during a round of golf. Fewer golfers understand the legal relevance of God's occasional answer when He replies with bolts of lightning. If He wants to play through, let Him.

Traditionally, an act of God is treated as the cause of an accident if it is a purely natural force that cannot be prevented by any amount of foresight and care reasonably expected of a defendant. This is legal shorthand to saying "it's not my fault." When the lightning is not foreseeable or preventable, the defendant is not liable. However, under New Jersey law, Spencer might recover from the Club if the Club were negligent. In this situation, the act of God does not shield the defendant from liability.

The appellate court reasoned that a defendant is not relieved from liability when the defendant is negligent. In such a case, the wrongdoer is not relieved from liability. This view of liability is reflected in the state's Model Jury Charge 5.14, which provides that:

> An act of God is an unusual, extraordinary and unexpected manifestation of the forces of nature, or a misfortune or accident arising from inevitable necessity

which cannot be prevented by reasonable human foresight and care. If plaintiff's injuries were caused by such an event without any negligence on the part of the defendant, the defendant is not liable therefor. However, if the defendant has been guilty of negligence which was an efficient and cooperative cause of the mishap, so that the accident was caused by both the forces of nature and the defendant's negligence, the defendant is not excused from responsibility.

The key to the legal puzzle is the defendant's conduct.[24] Thus, the case was sent back for a determination of whether the country club was negligent.

The appellate court usefully outlined its idea of the duty of reasonable care as it pertains to lightning. On the one hand, it said that all golf courses, at least in New Jersey, have a duty to post a sign that details what, if any, safety procedures are being utilized by the golf course to protect golfers from lightning. If there are no safety precautions, a sign must inform golfers that they play at their own risk and that no safety procedures are in effect. On the other hand, if a golf course uses a particular safety feature, the course owes golfers the duty to use it correctly. This means, for example, that if a golf course builds weather

---

24. Not all jurisdictions follow this approach to lightning strikes on a golf course. The Supreme Court of Tennessee declined to find that a state-owned golf course had the legal duty to protect golfers from lightning. Plaintiff's widow, who was suing because her husband had been killed by a bolt of lightning, alleged that the course was negligent in failing to erect lightning-proof shelters or in not having a warning system to vacate the golf course during electrical storms. The court held that the state's conduct did not fall below the applicable standard of care. It reasoned that lightning was such a highly unpredictable occurrence of nature that the risk to be guarded against was too remote to impose liability. Moreover, the court observed that dangers associated with playing golf in a lightning storm were obvious to most adults and that the plaintiff's husband could have reached the safety of the clubhouse in two minutes. *Hames v. State*, 808 S.W.2d 41 (Tenn. 1991).

shelters, it must build lightning-proof shelters. If it has an evacuation plan, the plan must be reasonable and must be posted. If it uses a siren or horn system to warn golfers of lightning, the golfers must be able to hear it and must know what the signals mean. Finally, if the golf course uses a weather forecasting system, it must use one that is reasonable under the circumstances.

Inside the Rules, Rule 6-8.a.(ii): "Discontinuance of play"

One does not have to be Ben Franklin or his namesake to know that metal golf clubs, golf umbrellas, and golf course open space can be dangerous when there is lightning. During the 1975 Western Open in Illinois, professional golfer Lee Trevino, affectionately known as the "Merry Mex," was hit by lightning. He famously thundered: "I should have held up a one-iron. Not even God can hit a one-iron."

Maussner v. Atlantic City Country Club, Inc. confirms the reminder. On the one hand, most golfers know that bad weather alone is never a good reason for postponing a round of golf. In fact, the rules confirm that "bad weather is not of itself a good reason for discontinuing play." On the other hand, the rules contain a common-sense exception. During competition, a player may unilaterally decide to discontinue play when there is a danger from lightning, and the player may do so without first consulting fellow competitors or the committee overseeing the competition. Playing on after play has been suspended by the committee may result in the recalcitrant player being disqualified. There is a more important point: If a golfer can hear thunder, there is a real risk of being struck by lightning. At least five percent of all lightning deaths occur on golf courses.

Hole Six

Federal:

Courville v. Comm'r, 71 T.C.M. (CCH) 2496 (U.S. Tax Court) (1996)

Golf and the Internal Revenue Service

Will Rogers remarked that the income tax has made more liars out of the American people than golf. Do you find this hard to believe?

William Courville was an optical engineer for many years. As a result of corporate downsizing at Lockheed Missile & Space, he was laid off from his engineering job. Following the loss of his job, he was faced with the decision of what to do with the rest of his life. For many like William, the answer was obvious: golf.

Now that he was unencumbered with his engineering job, William decided to pursue his life-long goal of becoming a professional golfer. He had played golf since he was a kid and had developed some talent for the sport. As an amateur golfer he carried a handicap of 5 and thought he could improve. He had distinguished himself by winning several local club championships, none of which, however, carried any prize money.

William set his sights on playing on the Professional Golf Association (PGA) Senior Tour, which is open to qualifying golfers who are fifty years and older. In order to qualify to play as a professional in a PGA Senior sponsored tournament, a golfer is required to qualify through a "qualifying school" (Q-school) for a tour card, to qualify for individual tournaments, or to establish a track record from the PGA tour indicating that he is a consistently strong performer. The likelihood of success is marginally better than winning the lottery. Each year, only eight golfers out of more than 300 qualify from Q-school. Only four golfers out of over 100 qualify for an individual tournament.

Undaunted by these statistics, William tried to qualify through the Q-school. He failed. He then tried to qualify through individual tournaments. The best he did was to make it as an alternate. William did not give up his dream. He continued to practice and take golf lessons from various players he met at the qualifying tournaments. He also sought counseling from a psychiatrist. The problem, in his view, was not his golfing ability, but his "thought process."

In 1995 William became a golf instructor in order to finance his continued effort to qualify for, and join, the PGA Senior tour. Golf became his life. When he was not teaching, he was either practicing or playing golf. Some might say, he was living the good life.

The Taxman Cometh

William's problem with the IRS started when he filed his 1991 Federal income tax return. On his tax Schedule C (Profit and Loss from Business) he reported zero income and over $16,000 in expenses. After 1991, he did not file a Schedule C for his golfing expenses. His explanation was straightforward enough to the average taxpayer: "I had no [wage or Schedule C] income, so how could I write off my expenses against no income?"

William detested record keeping. He kept no formal books or records; although he did keep an informal sheet of paper he labeled "Tax Info." It listed his golfing expenses for 1991, but, unfortunately for William, the amounts he claimed on Schedule C did not correspond with the amounts listed on his informal tally sheet. On the bright side, he did have some receipts for various expenses related to his golfing activities.

The Internal Revenue Service took an interest in William's tax returns. The IRS took so much interest in his tax situation that it honored him by naming a case after him: *William James Courville v. Comm'r.*[25] The honor of seeing his name in print was short lived, however. The Tax Court denied William certain deductions he claimed for his golfing activities and socked him with accuracy-related penalties equal to 20 percent of his tax underpayment.

The Internal Revenue Code contains rules for deducting business expenses. The Code provides that if an activity is not engaged in for profit, no deduction attributable to such activity is allowed.[26] The critical question in the Tax Court was whether William was engaged in the activity with the actual honest objective of making a profit. William had the burden of proving the necessary intent, which he failed to do.

Why was William unable to convince the Tax Court? In order to qualify an activity as a business and be entitled to business deductions, it is not necessary to actually show a profit. The taxpayer, however, must intend to make a profit. A proper business activity is one in which the taxpayer has the objective of making a profit, as opposed to the activity simply being a hobby or pastime.

The taxpayer's intent to make a profit is determined by

---

25. *Courville v. Comm'r,* 71 T.C.M.(CCH) 2496 (1996). The Tax Court's opinion was affirmed by the United States Court of Appeals, Ninth Circuit, in an unpublished opinion on March 13, 1997. *Courville v. Comm'r,* No. 96-70475 (9th Cir. Mar. 13, 1997).

26. Internal Revenue Code § 183 (a) and (b).

reference to a variety of criteria contained in the Income Tax Regulations. They include, for example, the success of the taxpayer in carrying out the activity, the history of income and losses, and the elements of personal pleasure or recreation from the activity. From a professional and financial standpoint, the court found that William's time and effort had been without much success. He failed to qualify for any PGA sponsored tournament, and had not earned any income as a professional golfer.

William clearly gains personal pleasure from playing golf. While there is no requirement that a taxpayer not derive pleasure from the activity, the elements of recreation and pleasure, when considered with other factors, are relevant to determining whether golf will be considered a legitimate business activity. In the court's opinion, William failed to carry the burden of establishing that his golfing activity was carried on with the actual and honest objective of making a profit.

Under the Internal Revenue Code, accuracy-related penalties can be imposed for the underpayment of tax attributable to the taxpayer's negligence or disregard for rules or regulations. The court observed that "petitioner's activity was far from being a for-profit activity." In addition to failing to keep regular books and records of his golfing activity, William failed to present any evidence to show reasonable cause as to why he should not be held liable for this type of penalty.

The term "rub of the green" is used by golfers to describe the situation when a ball in motion is accidentally deflected or stopped by an outside agency. William unhappily found out that the IRS is a formidable outside agency with the dexterous ability to rub the green out of a taxpayer's pocket.

Inside the Rules, Rule 9: "Wrong information"

In *Courville v. Comm'r*, the taxpayer gave the "wrong information" to the IRS. The rules governing the game also cover "wrong information." They are different for match play (Rule 9-2) and stroke play (Rule 9-3). The difference is based on the distinction that in match play only the player and his or her opponent are involved in the outcome of the competition, whereas in stroke play every competitor in the field has a direct interest in the outcome.

In match play, a player who gives the wrong information, such as the incorrect number of strokes taken (including any penalty strokes), to an opponent is penalized loss of the hole–unless the information is corrected before the opponent plays his or her next stroke. The penalty does not depend on whether the player is acting in good faith. Nor does the penalty depend on whether the player is responding to a question asked by an opponent or simply volunteering the information to be nice. Wrong information is wrong information, and it may affect what the opponent does next. And silence is not golden. In the unlikely situation that a player refuses to tell an opponent the number of strokes played, the player who remains mum also is penalized loss of the hole.

In stroke play, the rules are different. A player should inform the opponent of any incurred penalty "as soon as practicable." But no penalty is imposed for giving the wrong information to a competitor as to the number of strokes.[27] Other rules may apply, however. For example, submitting the wrong score, which is lower than actually taken, results in disqualification under Rule 6-6.d.

If the recorded score is higher than actually taken, the higher score stands under Rule 6-6.d. This type of over-reporting problem in stroke play happened to Roberto De Vincenzo at the 1968 Masters. Roberto and Bob Goalby were tied when the final putt found the bottom of the cup on the last day. Unfortunately, Roberto signed for a score that was one more stroke than he actually scored during the round. The additional stroke stood under the Rules, and Roberto lost the chance of playoff with Bob Goalby, who won the Masters by one stroke because of the error.

---

27. Decisions 9-2/3, 9-2/3.5, 9-3/1 (2006-07).

Hole Seven

Federal:

Pebble Beach Co. v. Tour 18 I, Ltd.,
155 F.3d 526 (5th Cir. 1998)

Copying Golf Course Design

Most people learn the meaning of the term "gimmie" at an early age. In golf, a gimmie generally refers to a conceded putt to a golfer who can't putt very well. But the term took on a new meaning in this golf case.

Dennis Wilkerson, Barron Jacobsen, and Jim Williams decided to build a public golf course in Humble, Texas, northwest of Houston. They knew the key to success was a well-designed golf course. Imitation may be the sincerest form of flattery, but it can sometimes get you into trouble, as the trio found out.

After a preliminary investigation, they determined that hiring a prominent golf course architect would not only be costly, it might not guarantee the success of their venture. Instead of hiring a course designer and planner for technical advice, the entrepreneurial trio hit upon an innovative idea—they would replicate the golf holes from famous golf courses throughout the United States and name their golf course "Tour 18."

As innovations go, the idea of replicating famous golf holes was to their way of thinking pure gold. Avid golfers the world over would be familiar with the prestige and difficulty of these famous holes. Indeed, some of the holes they picked have their own place in a golfer's vocabulary. Copying holes from the Blue

Monster (Doral), the Lighthouse Hole (Harbour Town), and the Church Pews (Oakmont) was part of the strategy to make Tour 18 a financial success. The course opened for business in late 1992.

The trio chose the copied holes based on several criteria, including the fame of the course, the fame of the hole itself, and their ability to replicate the hole after considering the geography, topography, and natural vegetation of their Texas property. The entrepreneurs considered hundreds of golf holes. They finally selected the following holes to copy at Tour 18:

Tour 18 Hole	Original Hole and Location
1	Harbour Town # 18 *(Hilton Head Island, S.C.)*
2	Bay Hill # 6 *(Orlando, Fla.)*
3	Pinehurst No. 2, # 3 *(Pinehurst, N.C.)*
4	Inverness # 18 *(Toledo, Ohio)*
5	Augusta National # 11 *(Augusta, Ga.)*
6	Augusta National # 12 *(Augusta, Ga.)*
7	Augusta National # 13 *(Augusta, Ga.)*
8	LaCosta # 4 *(Carlsbad, Ca.)*
9	Sawgrass # 17 *(Ponte Vedra, Fla.)*
10	Desert Inn # 10 *(Las Vegas, Nev.)*
11	Disney # 6 *(Orlando, Fla.)*
12	Colonial # 3 *(Ft. Worth, Tex.)*
13	Pebble Beach # 14 *(Pebble Beach, Ca.)*
14	Oakmont # 3 *(Oakmont, Penn.)*
15	Shinnecock Hills # 8 *(Long Island, N.Y.)*
16	Merion # 11 *(Philadelphia, Pa.)*
17	Oak Tree # 8 *(Edmund, Okla.)*
18	Doral # 18 (Miami, Fla.)

In addition to copying the above golf-hole designs, they used the service marks[28] of the golf courses in their Tour 18 advertising. To give golfers a heightened sense of vicarious enjoyment, signs at each hole told the golfers which replicated hole they were playing.

The Texas boys aggressively marketed Tour 18 as a golfer's dream. Advertisements were placed in local and national publications, such as the *Houston Chronicle, Golf Digest, Golf Houston, Corporate Golfer*, and in other promotional golf brochures and newsletters. One of the promotional brochures captures the dream they were selling:

Imagine yourself facing the awesome challenge of Augusta's famous Amen Corner, or contemplating Harbour Town's #18 complete with the red and white striped lighthouse to line up your tee shot, then finishing off with Doral's "Blue Monster" but before that, you'll be faced by some of the most renowned golfer's challenges, like Pinehurst #3 and many others. No this is not a dream, this is Tour 18. Tour 18 is the only golf course of its kind in the world. Each hole is a careful simulation of one of America's most famous golf holes. … Each hole features something unique … [a]nd with a little imagination you can almost smell the salty air and hear the seals barking as you play Pebble Beach's #14.

Though one might need an active imagination to "almost" hear the seals barking in a Houston suburb, Tour 18 was a financial success. In its first year alone, the golf course rewarded its

---

28. Service marks and trademarks are those words, symbols, phrases, or designs that the public associates with a single source of goods and services. The Lanham Act, a federal statute, protects against service mark and trademark infringement.

resourceful owners with $1.7 million in profits. Not about to let their idea go to seed, the trio quickly opened a second Tour 18 in nearby Flower Mound, Texas. They were Texans and thinking big. Plans were quickly hatched to expand the Tour 18 concept to Arizona, Georgia, and Virginia.

The owners and operators of Pebble Beach Golf Links,[29] Pinehurst No. 2,[30] and Sea Pines[31] were neither impressed by Tour 18's success nor flattered by the imitation. They responded by filing suit in federal court, seeking both damages and a permanent injunction against Tour 18 and its owners. They alleged, among other things, that Tour 18 violated federal and state law by using their protected "service mark" names without permission in Tour 18 advertising, promotions, and on-site signs, and also by copying their golf-hole designs without permission.

More was at stake to the plaintiffs than bruised professional pride. Tour 18 was a public golf course that charged each golfer $75 in green fees. By comparison, it was a bargain. That same golfer would have had to pay $245 in green fees at Pebble Beach, $164 at Pinehurst, and $145 at Harbour Town. To the plaintiffs, weekend golfing was big business, and they were not about to let an upstart Texas golf course trade on the goodwill and prestige of either their names or their golf-hole designs.

Plaintiffs' legal claims were complicated by some important facts. Pebble Beach does not feature its hole fourteen in

---

29. Pebble Beach is a California general partnership. It owns and operates five golf courses: Pebble Beach Golf Links, The Links at Spanish Bay, Spyglass Hill, Peter Hay Golf Course, and Old Del Monte Golf Course.

30. Resorts is a North Carolina corporation owned by Club Corporation of America. Resorts owns and operates a golf resort in North Carolina that includes seven golf courses, called Pinehurst and numbered 1 through 7.

31. Sea Pines is a South Carolina Corporation. It owns and operates Harbour Town Golf Links as part of its golf and tennis resort on Hilton Head Island, South Carolina.

any advertising materials, and it does not own a trademark, copyright, or patent for the design of this hole. Similarly, Pinehurst does not include hole three in its advertising, and also does not own a trademark, copyright, or patent for the design of hole three. Unlike Pebble Beach and Pinehurst, the imitated hole 18 from Harbour Town is featured in all its advertising materials. Hole 18 is widely known to golfers because of the distinctive lighthouse appearing in the background. However, Harbour Town does not own the lighthouse. Nevertheless, Tour 18's version of the lighthouse was an ersatz imitation of Harbour Town's neighboring lighthouse.

The Law

In a lengthy opinion, the federal district court entered an injunction against Tour 18 requiring it to "(1) cease using Pebble Beach and Pinehurst's marks, except to inform the public of the golf holes it copied; (2) cease using Sea Pines's marks and images of the lighthouse, without any exceptions; (3) remove the replicas of Sea Pines's lighthouse from both of its courses; (4) include a conspicuous disclaimer in all advertisements, promotional material, and informational guides; (5) maintain the disclaimers on the course; and (6) make no claims of use of original blueprints, maps, or other data in the construction of the course without a disclaimer." But the court denied plaintiffs' requests for damages, an accounting of profits, and attorneys' fees.

Tour 18 appealed. It challenged the district court's determination it had infringed and diluted the plaintiffs' service marks and Sea Pines's trade dress and that it competed unfairly. It also complained that the injunction was "overly broad, punitive, and vague." Not to be outdone, plaintiffs also appealed. Plaintiffs did not like the district court's finding that Tour 18 did not

infringe or dilute Pebble Beach and Pinehurst's trade dress or the denial of an accounting for profits and attorney fees.

The Court of Appeals upheld the district court's finding that Pebble Beach and Pinehurst's golf-hole designs were not inherently distinctive, and thus not protected by trade dress law. However, Sea Pine's golf-hole design, which was distinctive, was entitled to trade dress protection and that the lighthouse was a protected trademark. The court affirmed the determination of the likelihood of confusion from Tour 18's use of plaintiffs' marks and the design of the protected lighthouse hole, and that Tour 18's use of the marks did not amount to mere nominative use. On the matter of the remedy, it found that the injunction was appropriate, except to the extent that it prohibited nominative use of service mark belonging to plaintiff with lighthouse hole. It also found that the district court was correct in holding that the plaintiffs were not entitled to either an accounting of profits or an award of attorneys' fees.

1. Unfair Competition and Service Mark Infringement

The Lanham Act protects both consumers and producers of goods and services against unfair competition. The underlying theory of unfair competition is the unfair diversion of business outside the arena of normal competition. The same facts that support a claim for service mark infringement also support a claim for Lanham Act unfair competition.

To establish an infringement of a registered service mark under the Lanham Act, a plaintiff must first show that it has a valid service mark worthy of protection, and then prove that the defendant's use of the mark is likely to cause consumer confusion. Unregistered service marks also are entitled to protection under limited circumstances.

Pebble Beach and Pinehurst own registered service marks respectively to the names "Pebble Beach" and "Pinehurst" issued by the U.S. Patent and Trademark Office. The marks were therefore presumed valid. Sea Pines does not own a federally-registered service mark to the name "Harbour Town," so it sought protection as an unregistered service mark to the name and to the lighthouse image that was part of its logo. The name and lighthouse were sufficiently distinctive to warrant protection. Although the court found that each plaintiff had a service mark worthy of legal protection, that wasn't the end of the matter.

Defenses

After finding the service marks protected, the next issue was whether there was a likelihood of consumer confusion. The court found that Tour 18's advertising practices were likely to confuse purchasers. Yet one might reasonably ask, how could any golfer reasonably be confused? Even the most confused golfer would know he or she was playing golf in Texas, not in some other state and at a famous golf course.

The court reasoned that the possible confusion did not pertain to where the golfer was playing, but rather to the belief that Tour 18 had secured permission and approval from the plaintiffs to use their service marks in advertising and to use their names on each golf hole. The plaintiffs used both witness testimony and survey evidence to show this type of actual confusion by players. The potential for confusion was exacerbated by the similarity and overlap in advertising campaigns by the plaintiffs and the defendant, the fact the plaintiffs and the defendant both provided golf services, and the defendant's intent to take advantage of the plaintiffs' reputation, goodwill and service marks.

The federal law allows a defendant sued for infringement certain legal defenses. Tour 18 argued two defenses, namely, comparative advertising and their use of disclaimers to eliminate consumer confusion.

An imitator may lawfully use or copy another's product in comparative advertising so long as the consumer will not be confused. Tour 18 argued that it used the plaintiffs' service marks only to inform their golfers as to the source of the copied golf holes. Therefore, the defendant argued, Tour 18's use of the plaintiffs' service marks was for comparative advertising (fair use) purposes and thus lawful.

The court questioned what comparative advertising purpose was served by Tour 18's use of plaintiffs' service marks in the menu to the golf course's restaurant, including: the Harbor Town sandwich, the Pinehurst tuna salad, and the Pebble Beach French toast. Moreover, the court noted that Tour 18's prominent use of plaintiffs' service marks in its brochures, signs, advertisements and scorecards showed that Tour 18's purpose was not to inform its golfers, but to distinguish its own services from the services offered by the other golf courses. In the end, the court rejected this defense.

Tour 18 also argued that its disclaimers effectively eliminated any consumer confusion. In order for this disclaimer defense to work, Tour 18 had to show that its disclaimers were prominently displayed. The court also rejected this theory. Tour 18 presented no evidence that the disclaimers it used were actually effective in eliminating consumer confusion. Moreover, most of its advertisements did not contain any disclaimers, and those that did were obscure and in minuscule print, and thus not conspicuous or prominent—another legal whiff for the defendant.

2. Trade Dress Infringement

The Lanham Act protects unregistered "trade dress" when certain requirements are met. The term "trade dress" refers to overall appearance of a product, including its size, shape, color or color combinations. The trade dresses at issue were the shapes of the plaintiff's holes, their length and width, the placement and shape of bunkers and water hazards, and so on. Harbour Town made the additional trade dress claim that the design and appearance of the red and white striped lighthouse used by Tour 18 violated its trade dress.

To successfully prove a case of trade dress infringement under the Lanham Act, a party must demonstrate that (1) its trade dress is primarily non-functional; (2) the alleged infringement creates a likelihood of confusion; and, (3) the trade dress either is inherently distinctive or has acquired a secondary meaning. If upon seeing a product, a consumer immediately recognizes its source, the trade dress is inherently distinctive. By contrast, secondary meaning occurs when "in the minds of the public, the primary significance of a … [mark] is to identify the source of the product rather than the product itself." Secondary meaning has been acquired when the customer makes a mental association with a product's trade dress and source over an extended period of time.

Pebble Beach and Pinehurst claimed that defendant's replicating their golf-hole designs was trade dress infringement. Sea Pines argued that Tour 18's copying of its Hole 18 also was a trade dress infringement. The court rejected the Pebble Beach and Pinehurst claims that the designs were entitled to protection. They were not distinctive and had not acquired a "secondary meaning" with the public. The court did find, however, that Sea Pines's golf-hole design presented a valid trade dress infringement claim.

A particular golf-hole design is distinctive if it serves as a source indicator to the golf course. A hole design is a source indicator if a golfer is able to recognize the design and associate it solely with the original golf course. Nothing on the Pebble Beach or Pinehurst golf holes served as a source indicator. In fact, the court found that the designs were mere variations on common golf-hole designs. The court also concluded that the golf-hole designs did not have a "secondary" meaning, primarily because the advertising by Pebble Beach and Pinehurst did not focus on these holes.

In contrast, Harbour Town's Hole 18 was found to be distinctive. Hole 18 is inherently distinctive because it is the course's "signature hole" and acts as a source indicator to the golfing public. Golfers seeing the red-and-white-striped lighthouse at Tour 18 think of the Harbour Town golf course. Having found the Hole 18 design distinctive, the next issue was whether there was the likelihood of confusion. Since the court had already found the likelihood of confusion with regard to the service mark infringement, the court metaphorically pirated the same reasoning on the claim of trade dress infringement.

The court's service mark analysis suggests the difficulties lying ahead for plaintiffs claiming trade dress infringement. Almost all golf holes combine common features, such as bunkering and split-level greens. Thus, it may be difficult to establish the necessary level of distinctiveness that will serve as a source indicator in the overwhelming number of future cases. The requisite level of fame needed to establish secondary meaning is also likely to be problematic for establishing any protection for most golf holes.

The Remedy

The court did not find evidentiary support for the award of damages. Nevertheless, it enjoined Tour 18 from using the service marks "Pebble Beach" and "Pinehurst" in all contexts except use in comparative advertising that contains prominent and clear disclaimers. Although the court did not enjoin Tour 18 from using the Pebble Beach or Pinehurst golf-hole designs, it did enjoin Tour 18 from using a lighthouse that was confusingly similar to the trade dress lighthouse of Harbour Town Hole 18. Because Tour 18 could no longer copy Harbour Town's Hole 18, there was no need for comparative advertising. Therefore, Tour 18 was permanently enjoined from using the Harbour Town service mark for any purpose.

Tour 18 did not have to alter or change any of its golf holes. It is still in business and touts its golf courses as simulating holes from some of the greatest golf courses in America.[32] Thus, the case stands for the proposition that only limited protection is available for golf-hole design.

---

32. http://www.golfguys.net/golf-courses/Dallas/Tour-18-Dallas-Golf-Club.html

Inside the Rules, Rule 8: "Advice; Indicating Line of Play."

Pebble Beach Co. v. Tour 18 involves advice on copying golf-course design. The rules governing the game also regulate giving and asking for advice. "A player must not (a) give advice to anyone in the competition playing on the course other than his partner, or (b) ask for advice from anyone other than his partner or either of their caddies."[33] Advice is broadly defined as "any counsel or suggestion that can influence a player in determining the play, choice of club or method of making a stroke."[34]

At the 2007 Honda Classic, professional golfer Mark Wilson hit his tee shot on the fifth hole with an 18-degree hybrid club. Camillo Villegas was up next on the tee. Villegas asked his own caddie, Matty Bednarski, what club he thought Wilson had hit, which is allowed under the Rules. Bednarski said it was probably a two-or three-iron hybrid. Wilson's caddie, Chris Jones, volunteered it was an 18-degree hybrid. Jones's response violated Rule 8-1, which Wilson called to the attention of a Rules official upon completing the hole. Asking another competitor what club a competitor used to hit a shot also violates the advice rule. The penalty for the violation depends on the type of competition. In match play, the penalty is loss of the hole; in stroke play, it is "two strokes." Because of Jones' error, Wilson was subject to a two-stroke penalty that forced him into a playoff. But sometimes nice guys finish first—Wilson won the playoff.

Several important exceptions to the advice rule can apply. A player may ask for information about the Rules or about matters of "public information," including factual information

---

33. Rule 8-1.
34. Definitions, "Advice."

normally available to all players, such as the location of a yardage marker or sprinkler head. In addition, there are special rules on "indicating the line of play" both on and off the putting green. Before making a stroke on the putting green, a partner or caddie may indicate the line-of-putt to the golfer so long as the green is not touched to indicate the line. Touching the line-of-putt with a club or the flagstick violates the rule. In cases other than on the putting green (off the green), anyone can indicate the line-of-play, but no one may be positioned by the player on or close to that line while the stroke is being made. Also, any mark placed by the player to indicate the line-of-play must be removed before the stroke is made.

Hole Eight

California:

Morgan v. Fuji Country U.S.A., Inc.,
34 Cal. App. 4th 127 (1995)

Golf Course Liability to a Golfer

C astle Creek Country Club is located about forty miles north of San Diego, California. The golf course, owned at the time by Fuji Country USA, Inc., is designed so that trees divide the fairways of many holes. William C. Morgan, a retired businessman and member of Castle Creek Country Club, was a regular player at the course. He typically played there two or three times a week.

A stand of pines separates the fourth green and the fifth teeing area. The green and tee box are about forty yards apart. Several mature pine trees shade both the fifth-hole's teeing area and the adjacent concrete cart path. William knew that an errant shot from the fourth hole often got snared in the boughs of the pine trees. He also knew that golf balls occasionally sailed over the pine trees and landed on the fifth-hole teeing ground or surrounding area.

For protection from incoming wayward shots, he routinely would stand underneath the tree that offered maximum protection. The pine tree that provided William and other golfers with refuge from misdirected shots became diseased and the Club removed it. On various occasions after the tree was removed, William saw players standing on the fifth-hole tee box

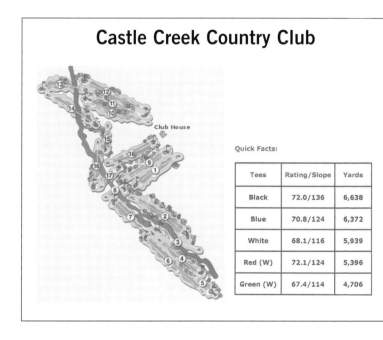

almost hit by the golf balls of players approaching the fourth green.

After hitting his tee shot on the fifth hole, William walked back to his golf cart, which was parked on the cart path. While putting his club away, he was struck by a golf ball hit by a golfer playing the fourth hole. The ball ricocheted off the cart path before hitting him on the head and injuring him. But it was no ricochet romance for William.[35]

William sued Fuji Country U.S.A. (Fuji) for compensatory

---

35. The song *Ricochet Romance*, written by Larry Coleman, Joe Darrion, and Norman Gimble, was a popular favorite in 1953.

They warned me when you kissed me your love would ricochet. Your lips would find another and your heart would go astray. I thought that I could hold you with all my many charms. But then one day you ricocheted to someone else's arms.

CHORUS: And baby I don't want a ricochet romance. I don't want a ricochet love. If you're careless with your kisses, find another turtle dove. I can't live on ricochet romance, no, no not me. If you're gonna ricochet, baby, I'm gonna set you free.

damages on the theory of negligence. Fuji responded by filing a motion for summary judgment. It claimed that William knowingly assumed the risk of being struck with a golf ball. The trial court ruled in favor of Fuji, reasoning that assumption of the risk operated as a complete bar to William's claim. Not liking this result, William appealed on the theory that the trial court incorrectly applied the doctrine of assumption of the risk. The court of appeal agreed and reversed.

The Defense of Assumption of the Risk

The basic idea underlying the law of negligence is reasonably straightforward. Conduct is considered negligent if it violates the standard established by the law to protect others from unreasonable risk of harm. There are defenses to a claim of failure to act as a reasonable person. One defense is that the injured golfer assumed the risk of the event that caused the injury.

The prevailing view is that voluntary participants in active sports assume all obvious and foreseeable risks of injury. A defendant generally has no legal duty to eliminate or protect a participant against the risks inherent in the activity itself. For this view to apply it must be clear that the person assuming the risk had actual knowledge of the danger and an appreciation of its character.

From the early 1990s California has adopted two variations of assumption of the risk. One type acts as a complete bar to recovery, which was the trial court's view, while the other type simply reduces recoverable damages. In the first type, called primary assumption of risk, the defendant has no duty to protect the plaintiff from a particular risk. Because no duty exists, the defendant has done nothing to warrant imposing liability.

The theory is that the plaintiff's actual knowledge and appreciation of the danger extinguish any duty the defendant might otherwise owe the plaintiff. Knowledge and appreciation of the danger are the keys to understanding the operation of assumption of the risk as a bar to recovery.

In secondary assumption of risk cases, the defendant owes the plaintiff a duty of care. Unlike primary assumption of the risk cases where no duty exists, secondary assumption cases are governed by comparative fault principles. This approach means that responsibility for the injury is apportioned based on the plaintiff's and defendant's relative responsibilities. In short, this type of assumption of the risk does not act as a complete legal bar to recovery. Rather, any financial recovery is reduced by the comparative fault of the plaintiff.

Fuji argued that the risk of being hit by a golf ball was obvious to William, so it owed him no duty. In other words, the case fit within the primary assumption of the risk category and it was entitled to win because assumption of the risk by William acted as a complete bar to his recovery.

The court of appeal disagreed. It held that cases between a golfer injured by a player in another foursome and a golf course are included within the secondary category of assumption of the risk. This means that Fuji owes William a duty of care to design and maintain the course to protect him from unreasonable risks of injury from errantly hit golf balls. More generally, golf courses have an obligation to design and maintain the golf course to minimize the risk that a golf ball will hit any player. Assumption of the risk might reduce the plaintiff's recovery, but not bar it.

The court of appeal concluded that Fuji was not entitled to win the case as a matter of law because the matter was within the secondary category of assumption of the risk, and thus the trial court erred. As a result, William was allowed to proceed with proving that the layout of the fourth and fifth holes and the removal of trees increased the risk of injury to him. Whether Fuji met its duty to provide a reasonably safe golf course was a question for a jury to decide on remand to the trial court.

It might have been an entirely different matter had the claim been against another golfer, rather than the golf course. Had the defendant been another golfer, the primary assumption of the risk standard arguably would foreclose liability, at least in California, on the theory that getting hit by ball is an inherent risk of playing golf.[36] A golf shot that does not behave properly is an inherent risk of the game. The fact that golfing etiquette calls for shouting the warning "fore" should not create a duty towards fellow golfers nor should failure to comply with this rule of etiquette constitute intentional or willful misconduct triggering liability.

Inside the Rules, Rule 19-1:
Ball in Motion Deflected or Stopped
by Outside Agency ("Rub of the green")

Golfers must take the good and bad bounces of the golf ball in stride. The rules use the quaint phrase "rub of the green" to describe the situation when a ball in motion is accidentally deflected or stopped by an "outside agency."[37] The term "outside agency" is defined as something that is "not part of the match or, in stroke play, not part of the competitor's side." It includes,

---

36. In June 2007, this question was argued before the California Supreme Court in *Shin v. Ahn*, 51 Cal. Rptr.3d 430 (2006) (pet. for review granted).

37. Another quaint phrase is "through the green." It refers to the entire area of the course except the teeing ground and putting green of the hole being played, as well as all hazards on the course.

for example, such things as sprinkler heads, yardage markers, trash cans, but expressly excludes wind and water. It does not, however, include calling on God to improve one's shot while the ball is still in motion.

In *Morgan v. Fuji Country U.S.A., Inc.*, William would be an "outside agency." The player who hit him would be required to play the ball where it came to rest without any penalty under the rules. But there are two notable exceptions to the "play-it-where-it's-found" rule. One deals with the ball coming to rest in or on any moving or animate object. This situation, for example, would occur had the ball hit William and then landed in his golf cart. The ball is replaced as nearly as possible to the spot where the interference occurred. The player does not have to hit the ball out of the golf cart. The other outside-agency interference exception to a ball in motion occurs after a stroke occurs while putting on the green. This situation would occur, for example, should a putted ball (ball in motion) be deflected by a squirrel (outside-agency) dashing across the green. The stroke is canceled, the ball replaced, and the stroke replayed. Special rules apply when the accidental deflection occurs by the player, partner, or equipment,[38] as well as when the deflection occurs by an opponent or opponent's equipment.[39]

---

38. Rule 19-2.
39. Rule 19-3.

Hole Nine

California:

*Bernardo Heights Country Club v.
Community Association of Bernardo
Heights (D024460), Fourth Appellate
District, (April 6, 1998)*

A Different Type of Lateral Hazard:

Private Easements on Golf Course Property

Stephen Colbert, comedian, satirist, and host of the popular television program *The Colbert Report*, popularized the word "truthiness." The term, which was voted 2005 Word of the Year by the American Dialect Society, refers to the quality of concepts or facts one wishes to be true, rather than those which are known to be true. Criminal lawyers are especially familiar with the idea.

Stephen often says, "I don't trust books; they are all fact and no heart." His dislike of facts was in full bloom when he dead-panned to Jon Stewart, another popular comedy channel personality, that his upcoming vacation plans included "an intense seven-day investigation into the Royal St. Barts Golf Club and Resort," the Caribbean's' ritziest fictional retreat. Nevertheless, it seems fair to say that even comedians like golf and golf courses.[40]

The Bernardo Heights Country Club ("Country Club") is a

---

40. For example, in a program segment called "The Word," Stephen reports "the conservationistas say calling a golf course a wetland is dishonest, and that without golf courses, wetland acreage is actually down by half a million acres. (500,000 handicap). ... Everyone wants a really nice golf course." www.colbertondemand.com/videos/The_Colbert_Reports/Colberts_The_Word_Birdie.

private golf course situated near San Diego, California. It may not be as ritzy as the Royal St. Barts, but it is a real nice place to play golf.

The course is located within the planned residential community of Bernardo Heights. As is common with such planned developments, the developer, in this case Genstar Development, Inc., created a homeowner's association ("Association") to operate and maintain the community in accordance with the provisions contained in a master declaration of covenants, conditions and restrictions (CC&Rs).

The CC&Rs govern all of the property of Bernardo Heights, including the golf course. In what many might consider Dickensian legalese, the CC&Rs provided:

> All of the property in the Community shall be owned, held, conveyed, encumbered, used, occupied and improved subject to the easements, liens, covenants, conditions and restriction *stated in this Community Declaration* (italics added for emphasis). ... All of the easements, liens, restrictions and covenants hereof are equitable servitudes and shall run with the title to said real property and shall be binding on all parties having or acquiring any right, title or interest therein or thereto and shall be for the benefit of each Owner of any portion thereof and inure to the benefit of and binding upon each successor in interest of such Owners.

In 1986, Genstar Development sold the golf course to the Bernardo Heights Country Club. Between the signing of the deed and its recording, Genstar granted the Association several "in gross" (personal) easements over the slope-areas adjoining the golf course. In simple terms, this meant that the Association had a legal right to use the slopes. The golf course had the legal title to the slopes, but the slopes were subject to the Association's right of use.

At the time the easements were conveyed, Genstar wore the hat of both the grantor and the grantee because the Association was still under Genstar's control as the developer. The Association did not assume majority control until 1988, some two years after the sale.

The easements were for the purpose of providing irrigation and maintenance of the slopes. From the Association's perspective, both a benefit and burden attached to the easements. On the one hand, the Association received the benefit of aesthetically pleasing and stable slopes, some of which were adjacent to and viewed by individual homeowners living within the residential community. The easement allowed the Association to go on the property owned by the golf course to maintain and irrigate the slopes. On the other hand, the Association was burdened with the financial obligation to maintain and irrigate the easement area. In 1992, the Association said this cost was running about $20,000 a year.

In 1994, the Association determined that the cost of maintaining and irrigating the easement exceeded its benefit. The Association wanted out of this burden. It filed a legal notice of abandonment of the easements and stopped maintaining and irrigating the slopes. If effective, the Country Club would have had to assume these obligations, which it resisted. With Genstar out of the picture, the Country Club sued the Association to enforce the agreement.

Abandonment

Under principles of contract law, a properly executed contract normally binds only the parties to the contract. A contract normally does not bind third persons who are not parties to the

contract. You might think of it in terms of not being bound by a bet on the golf course unless you agree to it.

In matters involving real property, this principle has been adjusted to meet society's needs. It is often desirable to create obligations that are binding on parties who were not parties to the original contract. Thus, for example, if a real estate developer agrees with a purchaser that the property should be used only for residential purposes, normally it is important that this residential use restriction also apply to all subsequent purchasers of the property. The objective of the parties is to restrict the property to residential use regardless of who may own it in the future.

If the promise binds whoever owns the land, it is said by lawyers to "run with the land." This phrase is descriptive of the fact that the promise binds subsequent purchasers. To ensure that subsequent purchasers have notice of the promise, the agreement is recorded in a master declaration of CC&Rs, which is available for public inspection. Traditionally, the promises are analyzed under the law of real covenants when the claim is for money, and under the law of equitable servitudes when the claim is for injunctive relief.

How may real property interests be terminated? The answer depends on the nature of the property interest. Abandonment of an easement occurs when the holder of the easement manifests the intent to abandon it.

The Superior Court of San Diego County granted the Association's motion for summary judgment affirming its right to abandon the easement. The trial court also found that the deeds of easement did not create covenants or equitable servitudes. Moreover, even if the deeds did, they were not legally binding on the Association.

The Country Club appealed to the Fourth Appellate District, which affirmed the judgment in an unpublished opinion. The Country Club argued that the Association could not legally abandon its obligation to maintain the slopes because the "deeds of easement" created a binding covenant or equitable servitude. Simply put, the Country Club argued that the legal rules concerning abandonment of an easement did not apply, and that the Association couldn't simply abandon its obligations.

The appellate court rejected this argument. It reasoned that the conveyances creating the interests were personal to the Association, and thus did not resemble covenants or equitable servitudes that bind third parties. The court reasoned:

> Because the deeds of easement did not create a covenant running with the land or an equitable servitude binding on the members of the Community Association and their successors in interest, Community Association was entitled to treat them as that which they purported to be—deeds of easement subject to extinguishment by release and abandonment.

The court examined the documents creating the easements and found that nothing in them foreclosed abandonment. It further held that the Association properly recorded notices of abandonment as to each of the slope easements. The court relied on the traditional theory that an easement may be terminated through abandonment.[41] Once the easement was extinguished, this left the Country Club with the unencumbered title to the slopes and the Association without any continuing obligation to maintain or irrigate them.

A real covenant or equitable servitude may be terminated by a written release from the benefit holder, but one cannot unilaterally slip out from under a burden. Therefore, had the court accepted the Country Club's characterization of the Association's interest as a covenant or equitable servitude, which it did not, the Association would not have been able to unilaterally abandon the burden of maintaining and irrigating the slopes without legal consequence. The Country Club would have been entitled to claim damages or injunctive relief for the Association's breach.

Inside the Rules, Rule 27: "Abandonment of a provisional ball"

Bernardo Heights Country Club v. Community Association of Bernardo Heights deals with the requirement of intent and the law of abandonment. The approach to abandonment is markedly different under the rules governing the game.

Before leaving the teeing ground, a player may play a "provisional ball" for a ball the player thinks has been hit out-of-bounds or lost outside a water hazard. The Rules require a player to return to the original spot when a ball is actually hit out of bounds or lost outside a water hazard. In order to save the time

---

41. The court of appeal observed that "[t]he issue of whether the deeds of easement evidence a contract between the parties is not before us in this appeal."

required to go back to the original spot to hit another ball, the Rules allow a player to hit a "provisional ball." Before hitting, the player must announce he or she is hitting a "provisional ball."

If it subsequently turns out that the original ball is not lost or out-of-bounds, the player must abandon the "provisional ball" and play the original ball. If a player doesn't abandon the "provisional ball" as required by the Rules, the player is penalized for playing the "wrong ball" under Rule 15.

A related aspect to abandonment of a provisional ball is found in the definition of a "lost" ball. If a ball, for example, is not found by a player within five minutes of searching for the wayward ball, it is treated as "lost," and must be abandoned. Although the law generally requires the intent to abandon a property right, the definition of a "lost" ball does not.

Hole Ten

Federal:

Wilson Sporting Goods v. David Geoffrey & Associates d/b/a/ Slazenger, and Dunlop Slazenger Corp. aka Dunlop Sports Corp., 904 F.2d 677 (Fed. Cir. 1990)

Patent Protection of Golf Ball Design

The golf ball industry is big business. Several years ago the golf ball market was estimated to be $1.4 billion worldwide. It should not be surprising that companies have a strong economic incentive to protect patented golf ball innovations, as well as other golf-related patents, from infringement.[42]

Over the years, inventors have experimented with numerous golf ball designs. Most designs are proposed within the limits of U.S.G.A. Rule 5-1, which sets the specifications for minimum size, maximum weight, spherical symmetry and other golf ball physical characteristics.[43]

---

42. Law suits involving patent claims in the golf industry are common today. In early 1998, for example, the following infringement lawsuits were pending: *Callaway v. Spalding* over Spalding's System C golf ball; *Callaway v. Wilson* over the Wilson Staff Titanium driver's alleged violation of its bore-through hosel patent; *GolfGear International v. McHenry Metals* for the claimed violation of insert-technology patents; *Titleist vs. Kent Graphtec* for knock-off putters; *Softspikes v. Etonic* for cleat-design patent infringement; and *Adams Golf v. Nickent Golf* for the alleged infringement of its Tight Lies head-design for its fairway woods.

43. Using U.S.G.A. testing equipment, conforming golf balls currently can be no smaller than 1.68 inches in diameter, no heavier than 1.62 ounces, no faster than 250 feet per second (plus a 2 percent tolerance), and not cover an average distance in carry and roll exceeding 280 yards (plus a 6 percent tolerance). The U.S.G.A. has expressed concern that driving distances on the PGA Tour have increased from 260 yards to 269 yards in the last five years, with some pros driving further than the tolerance limit of 296.8 yards.

Today manufacturers are introducing golf balls featuring titanium, tungsten, or magnesium powders mixed into the cover or core. Before these and other advances in technology found their way into the market, golf ball manufacturers focused on improving balls by varying the dimple design on the cover of the ball. The dimples on the cover affect its aerodynamic drag and lift, and thus influence both distance and control.

The Basics of Patent Law

The U.S. Constitution authorizes Congress to establish a patent system to promote the progress of science and useful arts by giving authors and inventors the exclusive right to their respective writings and discoveries for a limited time. Pursuant to this authority, Congress has established a statutory system for the issuance and protection of patents. A federal patent gives the patentee the right to prevent others from making, using, or selling the patented invention without the patent holder's consent. Patents are now protected from infringement by federal law for a period of twenty years from the date of filing, not issuance.

To get a patent, the applicant must apply to the U.S. Patent and Trade Mark Office. The patent application must describe the invention by written specification. This specification is a critical part of the patent process because it gives the public, as well as the patentee, notice as to what is protected. The written specification typically consists of various standard parts, such as a background, a summary, and one or more claims, which delineate the elements and limitations to the invention.

To be patentable, the invention must be distinguishable from the prior art by being both novel[44] and non-obvious.[45] It

---

44. 35 U.S.C. §§ 102(a), 102(e) & 102(g). A patent is not obtainable if the invention is not "new."

45. 35 U.S.C. § 103.

must be an advancement beyond the prior art, which is generally defined as the knowledge available at a given time to a person of ordinary skill in the art. If it is not, the invention is not entitled to patent protection. The determination of whether a patent is obvious, and thus not protected, is one of the most litigated issues in patent law.

A patent infringement claim may be formulated as a literal infringement or as an equivalent infringement. Where the invention is a device, the plaintiff-patentee must establish that the infringer "makes, uses or sells" a device that includes each of the elements identified in the patent. Proving a literal infringement is often difficult when minor variations to the invention have been made by the alleged infringer. Clever infringers often attempt this ploy to avoid infringement.

When it is not possible to prove a literal claim, the plaintiff still may be entitled to protection. If the infringing product appropriates the essence of the patented invention, the doctrine of equivalents may apply to give the patentee protection from infringement.

The Dispute

In *Wilson v. Dunlop*, the federal courts grappled with the scope of patent protection for dimple design. The case, which was tried in the United States District Court of South Carolina, was based on the theory that Dunlop infringed Wilson's 168 patent under the doctrine of equivalents. The jury held that four of Dunlop's golf balls (the Maxfli Tour Limited MD, the Maxfli Tour Limited HT, the Slazenger Interlock 480 Surlyn, and the Slazenger Interlock 480 Balata) infringed Wilson's patent.

The United States Court of Appeals, Federal Circuit, reversed the decision in favor of Wilson. Although Dunlop raised various issues on appeal, the critical question was the correct application of the doctrine of equivalents. The Federal Circuit found that the range of asserted equivalents made by Wilson encompassed the prior art. The Federal Circuit reversed the trial court's determination of infringement on the theory that Wilson's patented ball would have been obvious in view of the prior art.

Wilson's Golf Ball Patent

Wilson's patent covered a certain configuration of dimples on a golf ball cover.[46] The patented location of the dimples was designed to create a symmetrical distribution to enhance the flight performance of the ball. Wilson, which sells such well-known balls as ProStaff and Ultra, held a patent for the configuration issued by the U.S. Patent and Trademark Office.

Generally speaking, the dimples described in the Wilson patent are arranged by dividing the cover of a spherical golf ball into 80 imaginary spherical triangles. Then the dimples, typically several hundred, are placed into strategic locations in the triangles.[47]

---

46. Claim 1 of the Wilson patent 168 reads:

1. A golf ball having a spherical surface with a plurality of dimples formed therein and six great circle paths which do not intersect any dimples, the dimples being arranged by dividing the spherical surface into twenty spherical triangles corresponding to the faces of a regular icosahedron, each of the twenty triangles being sub-divided into four smaller triangles consisting of a central triangle and three apical triangles by connecting the midpoints [of the sides] of each of said twenty triangles along great circle paths, said dimples being arranged so that the dimples do not intersect the sides of any of the central triangles.

47. For those interested in the technical aspects, the triangles are constructed as follows. First, the ball is divided into an imaginary "icosahedron," Figure 1. The golf ball is completely covered by 20 imaginary equilateral triangles, five of which join tips at each pole of the ball and ten of which surround its equator. Second, the midpoints of each of the sides of each of the 20 icosahedral triangles are located, marked as "Xs" on Figure 2. Third, the midpoints are joined, thus subdividing each icosahedral triangle into four smaller triangles. The central sub-triangles are referred to in the patent claims as "central triangles" ("A" in Figure 3), whereas the three sub-triangles surrounding each central triangle are referred to as "apical triangles." The latter are so

The Prior Art

Patent law precludes an inventor, such as Wilson, from obtaining a patent if the difference between the ball sought to be patented and the prior art is such that the ball would be obvious to one of ordinary skill in the art of golf-ball design. Dunlop could successfully defend the infringement claim by showing that the plaintiff's patent was invalid as being unpatentable in light of prior art, notwithstanding the issuance of what appeared to be a valid patent.

In order to determine whether Wilson's claim was protected, the Federal Circuit embarked on a historical review of golf-ball patents and design. The court found that the most pertinent

---

named because each of them contains an apex or tip of the larger icosahedral triangle. The resulting 80 imaginary triangles on the golf ball are shown in Figure 3. Critically important are the light lines which join the midpoints. As can be seen from Figure 3, they form the arcs of circles on the ball which pass completely around the widest part of the ball. There are six such circles, referred to in the patent as "great circles."

Figures 1, 2, 3

In discussing the technology associated with Wilson's claim, the court of appeals observed:

> All of the claims of the '168 patent require this basic golf ball having eighty subtriangles and six great circles. Particular claims require variations on the placement of dimples in the triangles, with one common theme—the dimples must be arranged on the surface of the ball so that no dimple intersects any great circle. Equivalently stated, the dimples must be arranged on the surface of the ball so that no dimple intersects the side of any central triangle. See Figure 4, below. When the dimples are arranged in this manner, the ball has six axes of symmetry, compared to prior balls which had only one axis of symmetry.

This was Wilson's view of the prior art, which was disputed by Dunlop. The parties agreed, however, that every golf ball has at least one great circle which is not intersected by dimples. It is the "mold parting line," a seam around the ball which is created where the two halves of the mold used to make the ball are joined.

Figure 4

prior art was a 1932 British patent granted to a man named Mr. Pugh. His invention was described in the following way:

> A method of distributing a pattern with substantial uniformity over the surface of a sphere, such as a golf ball, which consists in … form[ing] equilateral triangles in the case of the … icosahedron … , dividing the sides of the triangles so found into the same number of equal or substantially equal parts and finally joining corresponding points in each pair of sides of each triangle by a series of arcs of great circles, substantially as described.

The court also observed that the prior art included several patents issued to Uniroyal for a ball sold in the 1970s. The Uniroyal ball, the court found, was an icosahedral ball having six great circles with thirty or more dimples intersecting the great circles by about twelve to fifteen thousandths of an inch. It was beginning to look like Wilson's patent was obvious.

The Doctrine of Equivalents

The judicially created doctrine of equivalents operates to prevent a canny infringer from avoiding the law by adopting minor changes and substitutions as a means of avoiding a patent. When the accused product "performs substantially the same overall function or work, in substantially the same way, to obtain substantially the same overall result as the claimed invention", the doctrine of equivalents allows the patentee to pursue an infringement claim even though there is no literal infringement.

The Federal Circuit devised a "hypothetical claim test" to determine whether the Dunlop ball was substantially equivalent to the Wilson ball. The hypothetical essentially tests whether the prior art available at the time Wilson patented its ball would preclude an infringement claim. To show infringement by equivalence, Wilson had to prove that the hypothetical claim would have been patented notwithstanding the prior art. If the hypothetical claim would not have been allowed, Wilson would lose. In short, the test is simply, if Wilson could not have gotten a patent in the first place, it could not get back-door protection through the doctrine of equivalents.

The Federal Circuit explains the test this way:

> The specific question before us, then, is whether Wilson has proved that a hypothetical claim, similar to [its] claim 1 but broad enough to literally cover Dunlop's balls, could have been patentable ... . Thus, the issue is whether a hypothetical claim directed to an icosahedral ball having six great circles intersected by 60 dimples in amounts up to 9 thousandths of an inch could have been patentable in view of the prior art Uniroyal ball ... .

> We hold that these differences [from the prior art] are so slight and relatively minor that the hypothetical claim—which permits twice as many intersecting dimples, but with slightly smaller intersections—viewed as a whole would have been obvious in view of the Uniroyal ball. As Dunlop puts it, there is simply 'no principled difference' between the hypothetical claim and the prior art Uniroyal ball. Accordingly, Wilson's claim 1 cannot be given a range of equivalents broad enough to encompass the accused Dunlop balls.[48]

---

48. Dunlop's balls are icosahedral balls with six great circles, five of which are intersected by dimples. The balls contain 432 to 480 dimples, sixty of which intersect great circles in amounts from four to nine thousandths of an inch. In order for a hypothetical claim to Dunlop's balls, its limitations must permit sixty dimples to intersect the great circles by at least nine thousandths of an inch.

Following the *Wilson* case, the United States Supreme Court added some detail to the correct application of the doctrine of equivalents in *Warner-Jenkins Co. v. Hilton David Chemical Co.*[49] In order to ascertain whether inventions are equivalents, a comparative assessment may be made. Courts must exercise care in actually making this comparative assessment in order to avoid unintended consequences. A broad application of the doctrine has the potential of impermissibly expanding a patent beyond its original boundaries and harming innovation.

Innovation is important to the financial success of golf ball manufacturers. Their quest to secure patents on golf balls that travel longer, straighter, and with improved accuracy around the green is similar to a golfer's quest for a hole-in-one; that is: never ending.

Inside the Rules, Rule 5-3: "A ball unfit for play"

Wilson Sporting Goods v. Geoffrey examines the principles of patent law and the technical specifications for golf balls in terms of weight, size, and other technical details. Hundreds of golf balls are manufactured to conform to the Rules. Some golfers, for example, play "X-out" balls, which are usually marked by the manufacturer for painting or printing errors, because they are relatively inexpensive.[50] Other golfers only play "top-of-the-line" golf balls.

The Rules have a procedure for determining whether a golf

---

49. *Warner-Jenkins Co. v. Hilton David Chemical Co.*, 520 U.S. 17 (1997) (holding that the doctrine of equivalents must be applied to the individual elements of the claim, not to the invention as a whole).

50. Unless strong evidence exists that an "X-out" does not conform to the rules, a player may use an "X-out." Decision 5-1/5 (2006-07).

ball is fit for continued play during a round of golf. If the ball is visibly cut, cracked, or out of spherical shape, the ball may be determined unfit for continued play and replaced. If the ball is simply "scuffed" from hitting a cart path or other hard surface, the ball cannot be replaced until after the hole is finished. Although Rule 5-3 prohibits cleaning the ball being inspected, there is an important exception. A player is entitled to clean the ball when it is necessary to determine if the ball is actually unfit.[51]

The proper procedure for determining that a ball is unfit for play must be followed. Before lifting the ball to inspect whether it is unfit, a player must announce the intention to inspect the ball, mark the position of the ball to be inspected, and give the opponent the chance to examine the ball as well as observe the lifting and replacement process. Failure to follow "all or any part of the procedure" subjects to player to a one stroke penalty.

If a player wrongly substitutes a ball, the general penalty for breaching Rule 5-3 depends on the type of competition. In match play, the general penalty is loss of the hole; in stroke play, the general penalty is two strokes. If the player incurs the general penalty, no additional penalty for failing to follow the proper procedure is imposed under Rule 5-3.

---

51. Rule 25-1b.

Hole Eleven

Texas:

*Malouf v. Dallas Athletic Country Club,
837 S.W.2d 674 (Tex. Ct. App. 1992)*

Golf Course Liability to Neighboring Property Owner for Property Damage

Ever thought about buying a house on a golf course? Edward Malouf, Harry Hollander, and C.M. Presley not only thought about it, they did. The trio bought houses adjoining the sixth hole of the "Gold" golf course owned and managed by the Dallas Athletic Country Club (DAC). They learned first hand the hazards of living next to a golf course. Each suffered damage to his car or home from golf balls that were hit by unidentified golfers. Edward's Oldsmobile Cutlass stationwagon was damaged, Harry's Porsche was hit, and both C.M.'s Ford Mustang and fiberglass awning were pelted by stray shots.

They individually complained to DAC, but were told that the club's policy was not to reimburse neighbors for damage caused by unidentified third parties. The general manager for the club, Robert Jones, explained that DAC has a procedure for dealing with stray shots that cause damage. After receiving a complaint, the golf course management asks players in the likely foursomes whether anyone hit the offending shot. If someone comes forward and admits it, confession presumably being good for the soul, the DAC then either charges that person for the damage or puts the player and injured party together to sort the matter out. As most people might guess, this procedure does not always compensate those persons suffering the property damage. If you cannot find the responsible golfer, what do you do? You sue the golf course, which is what the plaintiffs did.

Edward, Harry and C.M. sued the DAC for their property injuries in a justice-of-the-peace court on the theory of trespass.[52] The trial court ruled in favor of the complaining trio, and the DAC appealed the decision to the Dallas County Court. After a new trial, the county court ruled in favor of the DAC and against the plaintiffs. The unhappy plaintiffs then filed in the court of appeals, which affirmed the county court.

The Intentional Tort of Trespass

The tort of trespass to chattels is committed by intentionally interfering with the plaintiff's possession in a way that causes harm. Trespass is considered an intentional tort to property, and it is commonly distinguished from negligence or nuisance. Trespass to land involves a physical invasion of real property, whereas trespass to personal property, such as the damaged cars, involves an interference with the owner's right of possession. In both cases, the plaintiff must prove the defendant intended the consequences that are the basis of the tort. In other words, the plaintiff must show that the golfer hit the ball with the intent that it wrongly enter the plaintiff's property.

---

52. Plaintiffs also claimed DAC was negligent, but the court rejected this claim because the DAC had acted reasonably to prevent foreseeable harm. Prior to the events that resulted in plaintiffs' claims, the DAC had extensively revised and redesigned the layout of fairway number 6, under the guidance of Jack Nicklaus, in order to minimize misdirected shots leaving the course. Golfers were required to aim left, away from the homes on the right. It also installed six-foot photina hedges and a fence as part of the redesign. Adjoining landowners also frequently argue for protection under the law of nuisance.

In the typical trespass case between an adjoining property owner and golf course, the golf course does not challenge the owner's assertion that the golf balls have landed on the property and caused damage. The reason is simple. Both the invasion and the damage are usually clear. Therefore, most golf-trespass cases depend on finding intent.

The court of appeals found no evidence to support the claim that the golfers who caused the damage intended that their golf balls enter the plaintiffs' property. Moreover, the record contained no evidence to support the claim that the DAC intended to commit an act of trespass violating the plaintiffs' property rights.

The court reasoned that although the golfers responsible for the damage intended to hit their golf balls toward hole number six, this intent did not violate any property right. Most golfers surely intend to stay on the fairway, instead of hitting a Cutlass, Porche, or Ford Mustang. The fact that the wayward ball might "slice" or "hook" onto plaintiffs' properties was an unintended consequence. Because plaintiffs failed to show that DAC or the individual golfers intentionally caused the golf balls to damage the plaintiffs' property, the appellate court upheld the trial court's finding that the DAC was not liable on the theory of trespass.

The legal point is straightforward. When a golf ball hit by a golfer unintentionally causes property damage, it will be difficult to base liability on the theory of trespass, especially when the suit is against the golf course. Other theories of liability might prove more successful.[53]

---

53. *See, e.g., Sierra Screw Products v. Azusa Green, Inc.,* 88 Cal. App. 3d 358 (1979) (holding an injunction requiring the owners of the golf course to redesign two golf holes to minimize the nuisance and resulting damage to adjacent landowners from the continuous intrusion of golf balls).

Nevertheless, a trespass to land claim might be successfully brought in certain cases. The essence of the theory of trespass to land is interference with the owner's right to exclusive possession and control of the land. No physical harm to the property is required. For example, if a golfer enters private property to reclaim an out-of-bounds (OB) ball, the golfer has committed a trespass to land, unless consent to recover the ball can be somehow implied. Property owners frequently post "keep out" signs to defeat claims of implied consent.

A golf course might be found jointly and severally liable if it could be shown that it somehow aided or ratified the acts of the trespassing golfer. It also might be liable if the golf course, through the actions of its employees, committed the trespass.

The next time you, or someone in your group, have the urge to retrieve an out-of-bounds ball by going on someone's private property, you might remember the law of trespass.

Inside the Rules, Section II: "Definitions"

In *Malouf v. Dallas Athletic Country Club*, the golf balls were clearly out of bounds (OB). As previously discussed, subsequent play of the next shot would be governed by Rule 27. Additional detail on the out-of-bounds Rule is useful because it is frequently encountered during a round of golf.

The OB line is determined by the nearest inside point in between two stakes or posts at ground level. Determining the actual line between the stakes or posts requires care. In some cases, it may be difficult to determine whether a ball is actually out of bounds by quickly looking at it. The process may be complicated because a ball is considered OB only when all of it is out of bounds. When OB is marked by a line on the ground, the line itself is OB, and the determination may be easier. The stakes, posts, and other markers used to indicate OB are usually colored white, but not always. The Rules don't specify the color.

A common question is whether a player can get relief from an OB boundary marker. An obstruction is anything artificial *except* "objects defining out of bounds, such as walls, fences, stakes and railings." Thus, no free-drop is available from the boundary marker even though it may otherwise interfere with a player's swing or stance.

Hole Twelve

PGA Tour, Inc. v. Martin,
532 U.S. 661 (2001)

The PGA Tour Meets the Americans with Disabilities Act (ADA)

The Supreme Court of the United States rarely considers cases involving golf. The Casey Martin case is an important exception. To some golfers, their greatest handicap is the ability to correctly tally up their score at the end of each hole. Other golfers face more serious challenges.

Casey Martin has a physical disability. He was born with a rare muscular and circulatory disorder in his right leg, known as Klippel-Trenaunay-Weber Syndrome. The primary vein in this leg is missing, and the smaller veins are malformed. Thus, the leg is malnourished and half the size of his left leg. Because the veins do not return blood from the leg, the blood pools there. The disorder causes Casey to limp with severe pain when he walks. Neither the existence nor the severity of his congenital disorder is in doubt. In fact, the problem is sufficiently severe that the progression of the disease may ultimately require the amputation of his leg below the knee.

The PGA Tour, a nonprofit association consisting of the best professional golfers in the world, has a "walking-only" rule

DAVID MAXWELL/AFP/Getty Images

Casey Martin

for most competitions, unless the PGA Tour Rules Committee grants permission to ride, which it rarely does. Whether this rule conflicts with the protections of the Americans with Disabilities Act of 1990 (ADA) was at the center of the litigation.

Casey would prefer to walk during tour competition, but it is too painful due to his disability. He needs to use a motorized cart to get from shot to shot. The walking-only rule forced him to sue the PGA Tour in Oregon federal court. His theory was that by not allowing him to use a motorized golf cart, the PGA Tour failed to make its golf tournaments accessible to disabled individuals in violation of the ADA.

Casey won the first round. The federal district court found that the ADA applied. It also held that allowing him to use a motorized golf cart would be a reasonable accommodation, and would not frustrate the purpose of the Tour's walking rule or alter the fundamental nature of professional golf tournament competition. Therefore, the Tour was directed to allow him to use a golf cart during Nike and PGA Tour events.

A three-judge panel for the Ninth Circuit Court of Appeals also ruled in favor of Martin. But events were happening elsewhere that confused the matter. Almost on the same day that the Ninth Circuit ruled, the Seventh Circuit held, in a remarkably similar ADA case, that the nature of the competition would be fundamentally altered if the walking rule were eliminated.[54] The Ninth and Seventh Circuits had different views on the nature of the game, the walking-only rule, and the application of the ADA.

The Supreme Court of the United States resolved the split between the Ninth and Seventh Circuits.

The Americans with Disabilities Act of 1990 (ADA)

In 1990, Congress enacted the ADA to protect the disabled from discrimination. It was designed to require the removal of barriers that prevent persons with disabilities from sharing in and contributing to the vitality of American life. The thrust of the law is to require businesses and public entities to provide reasonable accommodation for disabled persons unless the businesses or public entities can show that the accommodation would fundamentally alter the activity in question.

Martin argued in the district court that the Tour's "no-cart" rule violated Titles I and III of the ADA. Title I prohibits entities covered by its provisions from discriminating against qualified persons with disabilities in all employment situations. But an employer does not have to provide an accommodation, however, if doing so would result in an "undue hardship" for the employer.

Title III prohibits discrimination in places of public accommodation. It provides that "no individual shall be discriminated against on the basis of disability in the full and equal enjoyment of the goods, services, facilities, privileges, advantages, or accommodations of any place of public accommodation by any person who owns, leases, or operates a place of public accommodation." Title III does not apply if the entity can show that

---

54. *Olinger v. U. S. Golf Ass'n.*, 205 F.3d 1001 (7th Cir. 2000).

the modification would fundamentally alter the nature of the goods, services, or facilities or constitute an undue burden.

The Legal Issues

The Supreme Court considered two questions concerning the application of the ADA. The first is whether the Tour tournaments are subject to the ADA as places of public accommodation. The answer to this question depends on what Congress intended when it wrote the law. If the ADA applies, the second question is whether allowing a disabled contestant to use a motorized cart would "fundamentally alter the nature" of the competition by giving the contestant a special advantage over other competitors who must walk. If walking is considered an essential part of the competition, the Tour would be able to refuse Martin's request to use a cart.

The Tour argued that it was exempt from the ADA because it was a private club or establishment, not a place of public accommodation. It claimed that Congress never intended that a private organization, such as the PGA Tour, be required to change its tournament rules to accommodate a would-be participant such as Martin.

The Tour conceded that the ADA expressly listed golf courses as places of public accommodation. But it argued that a golf course is only a place of public accommodation when it is engaged in the ordinary and usual operation of selling tee times to the general public or providing spectator areas for tour events. In other words, the Tour maintained that the part of the golf course on which its tournaments are played — "inside the ropes"—were not places of public accommodation because the public was not allowed there.

The Tour also maintained that Title III applies to "clients and customers" seeking "goods and services" at places of public accommodation. Martin should lose, it argued, because he was not within the protected class of "clients or customers." As a playing competitor, Martin should be deemed an "entertainer" or provider of entertainment and outside the protection of Title III.

Rather than engaging in semantic gymnastics, the Supreme Court found Martin was in fact a "client or customer." Why? He paid the Tour money for the opportunity to compete. The Court reasoned "it would be entirely appropriate to classify the golfers who pay petitioner $3000 for the chance to compete in the Q-school and if successful, in the subsequent Tour events as petitioner's clients and customers."

But finding that the ADA applies to Tour competitions was only half the legal battle for Martin. Title III requires accommodation "unless the entity can demonstrate that making such modification would fundamentally alter the nature of such goods, services, facilities, privileges, advantages, or accommodations." The Tour claimed that allowing Martin to ride in a cart would fundamentally alter the nature of the professional competition, and therefore no accommodation was required.

The record on the nature of the game included testimony from some of golf's greatest players on the nature of the game. Arnold Palmer, Jack Nicklaus, and Ken Venturi each testified that fatigue can be a critical factor in a tournament, particularly on the last day when psychological pressure is at a maximum. Moreover, their testimony was that using a cart "might" give some players a competitive advantage over those players required to walk. Giving any one player a special advantage is inconsistent with the Rules of Golf. Interestingly, these golfing legends did not go so far as to express an opinion on whether allowing Martin to use a cart actually would give him a competitive advantage.

The Supreme Court determined that allowing Casey to use a cart would not fundamentally change the nature of the competition or give him an unfair advantage. It reasoned that the essence of the game of golf is the ability to make a good shot, not how one gets to the ball to make the shot. In the Court's view, how a golfer gets to the ball in order to make the shot arguably is irrelevant. The idea is to find out who is the best at getting the ball in the hole in the fewest number of strokes. This idea applies with equal force to the professional golfer on the PGA Tour as well as to the amateur.

The Court looked to the history of the game. It found that the tradition of walking existed until a practical alternative was introduced shortly after World War II when motorized carts were first marketed. Thus, "tradition" seemed a weak rationale for saying that walking is inextricably bound up in the essence of the game. In addition, the Court recognized that the sport of golf has regularly embraced advances in technology over the years. In a relatively short period of time, professional golfers have moved from wood clubs to steel clubs to titanium clubs to tri-metal clubs. The technological development of the golf ball used by professionals also suggests a willingness to embrace change.

What guidance do the Rules of Golf provide? The Rules do not state that walking is fundamental to the game. Moreover, when administratively convenient, the Tour has made exceptions to the no-cart rule. The power to do this is found in the Tour's Conditions of Competition and Local Rules, which provide that players shall walk at all times during the stipulated round *unless* permitted to ride by the PGA Tour's Rules Committee. In other words, when it is convenient to the Tour's Rules Committee, carts may be allowed. This often occurs, for example, in open and sectional qualifying tournaments. Carts are also frequently used to shuttle players between the ninth green and tenth teeing ground, and back to the teeing ground after discovering that a player's ball is lost or out-of-bounds. Professionals who play on the Senior Golf Tour also are given the option of using motorized carts.

Martin enthusiastically responded to his victory in the Supreme Court by saying, "Now I'm prepared to play golf, just like every one else." But the decision has produced mixed reviews from professional golfers and the media. In his dissenting opinion, Justice Scalia called the result a distortion of the text of Title III, the structure of the ADA, and common sense. He laments the Court's willingness to determine whether walking is "fundamental" to the game and nonessential when the Tour deems otherwise. He predicts that the case will be a "rich source of lucrative litigation."

The *Martin* case illustrates that the rules of sport competition are not beyond the scope of judicial inquiry. In the long run, whether the case broadly benefits sport competitors with disabilities is apt to depend on the willingness and determination of sports organizations to legally defend what is "fundamental" to the particular sport. With respect to golf, however, one can confidently predict there will be no groundswell to require professional golfers to carry their own golf bags and abandon the use of caddies to enhance the fatigue factor.

Now what? In May 2006, Martin was named head coach of the men's golf team at University of Oregon. He did not play in the Q-School in 2006, and therefore will have to rely on sponsors' exemptions and "Monday qualifying" in order to enter any subsequent tournaments. Regardless of his future success as a professional golfer, Martin has left his mark on American jurisprudence.

Inside the Rules, Definitions: "Equipment"

Martin v. PGA Tour, Inc. illustrates, among other things, the challenges some players have in walking a course during a round of golf. This challenge usually is not a problem because the typical golfer can use a motorized cart.

There are some special rules, however, involving golf carts. Under the Rules, a golf cart, whether or not it is motorized, is treated as "equipment." When a motorized cart is shared by two players, the cart and everything in it are considered the equipment of the player whose ball is involved. Should a player's ball accidentally be deflected or stopped by his or her equipment, a penalty is assessed under Rule 19-2. In match play the penalty is loss of hole; in stroke play it is two strokes.

There is an important exception, however. When a cart is being moved by one of the players sharing it, the cart and everything in it are considered to be that player's equipment so long as the operator is not a team partner. Therefore, no penalty would be assessed when the player's ball is accidentally deflected or stopped while the cart is being driven or moved by a fellow competitor.[55]

---

55. Decision 19/1 (2006-07).

Hole Thirteen

California:

Kurash v. J.C. Resorts, Inc. 00703109
Sup. Ct., San Diego, CA (1996)

Golf and the
Loss of Consortium

A below par performance is great during a round of golf. It's not so great in the bedroom. This case involves the latter type of performance.

August 29, 1995 was a great day for golf in Southern California. The weather was perfect for a day on the links. Stanley Kurash and three of his friends, Ed Brown, Bob Steele and Alexander Sirpis, decided to take advantage of a clear, calm and sunny day by playing golf on the North Course at Oaks North Country Club in Rancho Bernardo, California. The Oaks North Country Club is a popular executive-type course managed by J.C. Resorts, Inc.

The course winds its way through a well-manicured planned community. There are numerous trees on the course that beautify it and provide golfers, as well as adjacent property owners, with sanctuary from errant shots. The golf club's employees often trim the trees on the course with handsaws or pole saws. In addition, the club contracts with a tree-trimming service for additional maintenance.

Stanley and his friends golfed without incident through the eighth hole. The ninth hole is an uphill par four that runs parallel and adjacent to the driving range. It is separated by a line of

mature trees, mostly pines, from the driving range teeing area located on the right, which is out-of-bounds to players coming up the ninth fairway to the green. Stanley and Ed drove their cart to the right side of the fairway to retrieve a golf ball that Bob had inadvertently sliced. After retrieving the ball, Stanley approached his ball, which was also in the tree line.

Stanley heard a loud crack. Thinking that a golf ball from the driving range had hit the tree above his head, Stanley looked for the responsible golfer. There was none. Moments later, he heard a second, louder crack, which was followed by a large tree limb falling on him. The limb was some 12 inches in diameter and was estimated to weigh 750 pounds. Stanley was unable to extricate himself from the physical embrace of the limb until Ed lifted it high enough so that he was able to crawl from under it.

Stanley was taken by ambulance to a nearby hospital. He suffered various cuts, abrasions, and a broken nose. X-rays revealed that he had a broken left rib. He also suffered a bruised tailbone and other medical problems.

Stanley and his wife, Naomi, sued the golf course management. Among other injuries, Stanley claimed that he suffered sexual dysfunction from the fallen limb. He maintained that he was rendered permanently impotent, and claimed he was able to reach coitus with his wife of 53 years only after painful injections of Alprostil or suppositories. Both he and his wife were understandably unhappy.

Stanley said that J.C. Resorts was negligent in failing to properly trim the pine limb that fell on him. He argued the golf club was in control of the property and that its maintenance crew had inadequately trimmed and pruned the tree. This failure resulted in the growth of foliage at the end of the tree limb, creating a strain on the limb, which was relieved when the limb snapped unexpectedly and hit Stanley. While Stanley may have assumed some risk by playing golf, he did not, in his view, assume the risk of being struck by a limb from a failing tree.

J.C. Resorts argued that the trees were intentionally maintained in a dense fashion to serve as a safety screen against balls hit from the driving range striking players on the ninth hole. They also claimed they regularly inspected the trees, had no notice of any safety risk from falling tree limbs, and that the accident was caused by an act of God.

Consortium[56]

You might reasonably ask, "Why was Naomi able to make a legal claim against J.C. Resorts when it was her husband who was injured?" The answer lies in the mysterious ways of the law.

Naomi's claim was joined with her husband's. She maintained that his inability to function sexually was her loss as

---

56. The 4th edition of Black's Legal Dictionary defines consortium as the "conjugal fellowship of husband and wife, and the right of each to the company, co-operation, affection, and aid of the other in every conjugal relation."

well as her husband's. Naomi testified that while she knew that sex might not always be present in their marriage if they lived long enough, having it suddenly torn asunder from their marital relation by J.C. Resorts' failure to act prudently was more difficult than accepting it as nature's way. In response, J.C. Resorts argued that Stanley had erectile dysfunction before the accident. It also claimed that Stanley's age, 74, was the only other substantial factor causing his increased sexual dysfunction.

Historically, only a husband had a cause of action for loss of consortium when his wife suffered a non-fatal injury. A husband's claim was originally considered to be for loss of his wife's services. The theory was similar to a master's claim for loss of his servant's services in cases where the servant suffered physical injury. The claim was gradually expanded to include recovery for the "three Ss": society, services, and sexual intercourse.

In contrast to a husband's claim for loss of consortium, a wife historically had no reciprocal cause of action for her loss because she had no separate legal status. Without legal status, a wife had no analogous claim to her husband's. By the end of the nineteenth century, most states had enacted Married Women's Property Acts. These laws were enacted to remove a woman's legal disabilities that were based on the servile status as a wife and the absence of her independent legal status.

"For the Times They Are A-changin'"

Beginning in the 1950s, most states expanded the claim on a gender-neutral basis to permit wives to recover for the losses they sustained when their husbands were injured. Today, the overwhelming majority of states, either by statute or judicial decision, allow wives to sue for loss of consortium. The cause of action generally is limited to those in a legally recognized marital relationship. Unmarried cohabitants generally are barred, at least in most states, from suing for loss of consortium based on various public policy arguments. Thus, the loss of consortium is strictly a husband-wife "family affair."

A consortium claim is legally derived from the principal victim's claim.[57] In order to prevail for loss of consortium, the principal victim must first prevail. To avoid duplicating any award of damages, the loss of consortium claim is procedurally joined with the principal victim's claim. Therefore the claims are litigated together.

A claim for loss of consortium is compensable by a separate damage award either for the period of incapacity or for the spouse's life expectancy if the incapacity is shown to be permanent. After a five-day trial, the jury found for the plaintiffs. Stanley was awarded $55,000 to compensate him for his injuries. Naomi was awarded $5,000 for her loss of consortium.

Inside the Rules, Rule 28: "Ball unplayable"

In *Kurash v. J.C. Resorts, Inc.*, Stanley was pinned to the ground by a fallen tree limb. At the time of the accident, he certainly was in an "unplayable" position. Naomi also subsequently found him somewhat "unplayable."

In order to declare a ball unplayable, the player must first identify it as his or her own ball. During the U.S. Open at Pebble Beach in 1993, golfer Nick Faldo practiced his Tarzan-like skills by climbing up a tree to identify his ball in order to declare it unplayable. His feat is a useful aid in remembering the rule.

---

57. In *Hennessey v. Pyne*, William, Eileen Hennessey's husband, joined the litigation also alleging a loss of the three Ss.

Once properly identified, a ball may be declared unplayable by a golfer at any place on the course with one exception. That exception is when the ball is in a water hazard. But declaring a ball unplayable has consequences. The player suffers a one-stroke penalty.

After declaring the ball unplayable, the player has three options. First, the player may go back to the spot from which the last stroke was played and take a drop. Second, the player may drop within two-club lengths of the unplayable ball, but no nearer the hole. If the unplayable ball is in a tree or bush, the ball is dropped within two-club lengths of a point immediately below the unplayable ball.[58] The final option is a little more complicated. A player may draw an imaginary line between the unplayable ball and the hole, and drop anywhere on that line so long as the drop is no nearer the hole than where the ball lay.

It is possible to drop from one unplayable lie into a second unplayable lie triggering a second penalty, so care must be exercised before taking a drop under the unplayable-ball rule.

---

58. Decision 28/11 (2006-07).

Hole Fourteen

Colorado:

Price v. Wilson Sporting Goods Co., 2005 WL 1677512 (D. Colo. July 18, 2005)

A flying club head causes injury:

Defectively Manufactured Golf Clubs

I n the 2000 movie "Cast Away," Chuck Nolan, a harried Fed-Ex executive played by the actor Tom Hanks, winds up on a deserted island after a plane crash. His silent companion Wilson helps Nolan cope with his struggle to make it back to civilization. Wilson, you may recall, is the image of a face (complete with spiked hair) that Nolan paints on a Wilson beach volleyball. The volleyball arrives on the island courtesy of the same downed plane.

Whatever his shortcomings as a companion, Wilson certainly provided a memorable boost to the image of Wilson sports products. But this boost to the company's brand image suffered somewhat of a setback when Wilson Sporting Goods Company was recently sued in federal district court in Colorado for manufacturing a defective golf club.

David Price and his son were playing a round of golf when the accident involving the defective golf club happened. David's son swung a Wilson Ultra pitching wedge, which was purchased at a Target store. The immediate target for his swing was his golf ball, not his father. But when the head of the club separated from the shaft, David, who was standing approximately 20 yards to the side and 10 to 20 yards in front of the teeing ground, became the unintended target. The flying wedge-head hit David causing him severe head lacerations, a skull fracture, and momentary unconsciousness.

David sued Wilson Sporting Goods, Target, and True Temper Sports. He moved for partial summary judgment against Wilson Sporting Goods on his claims of strict product liability and negligence. The court upheld David's claim of strict liability. But the court ruled against him on the negligence claim because it raised, in the court's mind, factual questions, such as whether Wilson Sporting Goods should have foreseen that David would be standing in front of his son when he was injured. These factual questions were for a jury to decide, and thus not appropriate to resolve on the motion for summary judgment. The claim of negligence would have to be sorted out by a jury at trial.

David presented two experts to support his claim of strict liability, whereas Wilson Sporting Goods Company failed to disclose their experts in a timely manner in accordance with the Federal Rules of Civil Procedure. Wilson also failed to file a timely response to David's motion for summary judgment. Thus, David made the case for why he should prevail on summary judgment, while Wilson's attorneys presumably were out looking for the beverage cart.

David's two experts testified that the pitching wedge was defectively manufactured. They reported that the epoxy used to connect the golf shaft to the club head was not evenly distributed around the shaft. This failure weakened the bond between the two components and created the opportunity for abnormal stress on the club during use. To seal their testimony, they testified that the misapplication of epoxy was not in accordance with "good adhesive bonding practice" in the industry.

The experts also reported that the end of the shaft where it fit into the club head was not properly prepared. While some grinding of the shaft is necessary to promote the proper bonding to the club head, the grinding on the shaft of the pitching wedge was deeper than required. During the manufacturing process, the chromium plating on the shaft was completely removed. This exuberant grinding at the end of the shaft compromised its structural integrity and made it prone to stress fracture during the golf swing. Finally, there was evidence of a potential welding defect, which also suggested defective manufacturing.

The set of clubs, including the pitching wedge, was relatively new at the time of the accident. The defective club did not show any sign of improper use or abuse. Moreover, the defect was not readily observable because a fixed-plastic ferrule located immediately above the hosel hid the defects. As a result, the problem with the wedge was most likely from a manufacturing defect, and not from the use of the club.

Because this expert testimony was not contradicted by Wilson or its experts, all that remained was the application of the law of strict liability. The district court applied the law of Colorado, which has adopted the Restatement (Second) of Torts. Section 402A of the Restatement generally provides that anyone selling a product in a defective condition that is unreasonably dangerous is subject to liability for physical harm to the user or consumer. A product is considered unreasonably dangerous when a manufacturing defect creates an unexpected risk of harm to a person.

David was a regular golfer, and thus was a person who would reasonably be expected to use the pitching wedge or be affected by its use. The fact that David's son actually swung the club that caused the injury was not controlling. The court reasoned that David was a person who would reasonably be expected to either use the Wilson golf clubs or, as a result of sharing them with his son, be affected by their use.

Based on the evidence, the court held that reasonable people could draw only the following conclusions: the pitching wedge was defectively manufactured, the wedge was unreasonably dangerous to David, and the defect was the cause of his injuries. The Wilson Ultra wedge was a real "cast away."

Inside the Rules, Rule 4: "Clubs"

The golf club in *Price v. Wilson Sporting Goods Co.* was defectively manufactured. A special rule exists when a club is substantially damaged during "normal" play, which would have applied had David been able to continue his round of golf with his son instead of being rushed off to receive medical attention. The Rules state that the damaged club may be replaced when replacing it does not "unduly" delay play. But they also provide that the replaced club cannot be borrowed from another player playing the course.[59] If a club is broken or damaged outside normal play, such as in a burst of anger, the club may not be replaced.

The Rules also limit the number of golf clubs a player can carry during a "stipulated round" of golf. Since 1938, a player cannot exceed carrying fourteen clubs. If a player has more than the maximum allowed, the player is penalized. In stroke play, there is two-stroke penalty for each hole at which any breach occurred up to a maximum of four strokes. In match play, the match is adjusted by deducting one-hole for each hole at which the breach occurred up to a maximum of two holes.[60]

---

59. Rule 4-3.a.
60. Rule 4-4.

Regardless of whether one is a professional or amateur, it always pays to check before setting off on a round of golf. In 2001, Ian Woosnam was leading the final round of the British Open when his caddie, Miles Byrne, gave him the bad news after he nearly made a hole-in-one on the first hole:

Byrne: *You're going to go ballistic.*

Woosnam: *Why?*

Byrne: *We've got two drivers in the bag (this meant Woosnam had fifteen clubs, and thus had to call a two-stroke penalty on himself).*

His caddie was right. Suffering a temporary meltdown, Woosnam bogeyed two of the next three holes. He finished the Open tied for third.

The reason for the rule limiting the maximum number of clubs a player can carry seems straightforward. Without some limit, golfers would insist on carrying any number of specialty clubs to fit every imaginable situation, and golf bag manufacturers could not build large enough golf bags to carry the assembled arsenal of weapons. Fourteen was selected by the U.S.G.A. because it was considered a "standard set" of two woods, two wedges, a putter, and nine irons.

Appendix II to the Rules prescribe the general regulations for the design of clubs as well as technical specifications and official interpretations. A manufacturer that fails to submit a sample club to the U.S.G.A. runs the risk of a ruling that the club will be found to fail to conform to the Rules. A player using such a club runs the risk of disqualification for using a non-conforming club.

Hole Fifteen

Mississippi:

Dowdle v. Mississippi Farm Bureau Mutual Insurance Co., 697 So.2d 788 (Miss. 1997)

Insurance and Golf Cart Accidents

Fred Flintstone, the popular animated character, is known for bellowing the phrase "Yabba-Dabba-Doo." He is also a golfer.[61] Fred drives around the fictional city of Bedrock in his Flintmobile.[62] With a little imagination, the Flintmobile resembles today's golf cart, which is designed to carry two golfers and their equipment.

The most commonly used motorized golf cart is a four-wheeled vehicle powered by an electric motor or some type of combustion engine. Its maximum speed, usually around fifteen miles per hour, often is controlled by a governor that prevents the operator from going above a certain speed.

Of the millions of rounds of golf played each year, golfers use a golf cart about half the time. Given the frequency of use, it should be no surprise that golf carts may be involved in accidents resulting in personal injury. According to one report, about half of all golf cart accidents involve negligent driving or

---

61. As perhaps the earliest golfer, Fred recorded the first "eagle" by striking a Pterodactyl with his club in 2000 B.C.

62. A picture of the Flintmobile is available at http://rides.webshots.com/photo/2207795180030961650esbfxk.

cart maintenance. The other half involve claims of product liability for defective design or manufacture of the golf cart.

When an accident involves driver negligence, the injured person may sue the driver of the golf cart or the driver's insurance company if the driver has insurance. Alternatively, the injured person may make a claim against his or her own automobile insurance policy under its "uninsured motorist" provisions. Depending on the exact cause of the injury, a negligence claim might also be made against the golf course in its capacity as either the owner or lessor of the golf cart.

Archie Dowdle was injured by the negligent operation of a golf cart driven by Jimmy Berryhill, Jr., who was uninsured. Archie lived with his parents and was covered by his father's automobile insurance policy issued by the Mississippi Farm Bureau Mutual Insurance Company. Archie claimed that he was covered by the policy and entitled to recover pursuant to the uninsured motorist provision of the policy.

Golf carts as motor vehicles

A golf cart arguably meets the common dictionary definition of a motor vehicle—a vehicle with a motor in it. The insurance company was not persuaded that the golf cart was a motor vehicle for purposes of coverage, and refused to pay the claim. Archie sued. The trial court found the insurance company was entitled to prevail as a matter of law and granted it summary judgment. The appellate court affirmed, and Archie took the matter all the way to the Mississippi Supreme Court. His luck was no better there.

The issue before the Mississippi Supreme Court was whether the golf cart should be treated as a motor vehicle under the uninsured motorist provision of the policy or under the state's Motor Vehicle Responsibility Act.

The supreme court held that a golf cart is not a motor vehicle. The court first looked at the policy definition of "uninsured motor vehicle." It excluded "equipment designed for use principally off public roads." In addition, the policy defined "automobile" to exclude "all-terrain vehicles or any other recreation vehicle." The court found the language of the policy "clear, unambiguous, and easily understood." The court also consulted Mississippi's Motor Vehicle statute. It defines "motor vehicle" as a vehicle "designed for use upon a highway." Thus, the statute did not provide a basis for treating a golf cart as a "motor vehicle."

Although the court found the language of the policy clear, reasonable people might disagree with the court's attempt to analogize golf carts to all-terrain vehicles. ATV's are typically high-speed machines intended for use on all types of rugged terrain, whereas golf carts are low-speed vehicles used on cart paths and more benign surface areas. The handling and stability characteristics of the two vehicles also are quite different.

But the policy also excluded "any other recreational vehicle." Moreover, the court reasoned that golf carts were excluded under the terms of the policy because they are designed primarily for use "principally off public roads." Golf carts used while playing golf are intended only for limited use on roadways with other motor vehicles. While Archie's witnesses submitted affidavits saying that the golf carts were used "from time to time" on the public roads, the affidavits did not help because the policy excludes equipment used "principally off public roads."

Dowdle v. Mississippi Farm Bureau Mutual Insurance Co. appears consistent with the view that golf carts are not typically used on roads and highways, and thus are outside the financial responsibility and no-fault coverage provisions of

117

automobile insurance. But some cases have treated golf carts as being within the definition of motor vehicle.[63]

Courts generally have had some difficulty in interpreting the scope of the term "motor vehicle."[64] The issue of insurance coverage for golf cart operation is apt to take on continuing importance in the future. One reason is that golf carts are being used increasingly for multiple purposes on and around golf courses and golf course communities.

The possibility of federal action may affect future judicial decisions on the scope of insurance coverage. If the National Highway Traffic Safety Administration succeeds in imposing federal regulations requiring certain golf carts to be equipped with seat belts, turn signals, windshields and other safety devices, courts may be more willing to classify golf carts as motor vehicles for insurance purposes. You can bet that the insurance companies will keep track of these developments, and tailor their coverage accordingly.

Inside the Rules, Rule 12-2: "Identifying the ball"

Dowdle v. Mississippi Farm Bureau Mutual Insurance Co. involves the importance of the insured identifying the exclusions

---

63. *Del E. Webb Cactus Dev. v. Jessup*, 863 P.2d 260 (Ariz. 1993) (holding incidental use of golf carts to cross public roads was "operation" of vehicle sufficient to subject lessor of carts to registration and liability insurance requirements for motor vehicles). *See also Coffey v. State Farm Mut. Auto. Ins. Co.*, 412 N.W.2d 281 (1987) (holding a golf cart to be a motor vehicle when being driven in a private subdivision by an intoxicated driver). *But see Ebernickel v. State Farm Mut. Auto. Ins. Co.*, 367 N.W.2d 444 (Mich. 1985) (requiring that an accident actually occur on public road).

64. Debts are non-dischargeable if they arise out of the debtor's operation of a "motor vehicle" while intoxicated under the Bankruptcy Code. The federal courts have split on whether motorboats are "motor vehicles" for purposes of applying the provision. *Compare Boyce v. Greenway*, 71 F.3d 1177 (5th Cir. 1996) (motorboats are not "motor vehicles") *with Willison v. Race*, 192 B.R. 949 (W.D. Mo. 1995) (motorboats are "motor vehicles").

to an insurance policy. Identification is also important in golf. A player must be able to identify his or her golf ball before hitting it. If a player cannot, the ball is treated as "lost" under the Rules.

In March 1999, Nick Faldo was disqualified from the Players Championship during the final round when he failed to first identify his ball when it got stuck in a palm tree at the sixth hole. Faldo was incorrectly advised by Corey Pavin that he could drop under the tree for a one-stroke penalty without identifying his ball. Faldo finished the hole and was disqualified. The ball should have been played as a lost ball. Pavin reported that the parting with Faldo after the round was amicable.

In order to be able to recognize one's own ball, a player should put some type of identifying mark on it. Even when the ball is marked, it is sometimes difficult to identify the ball as the player's own. This problem might occur, for example, when the ball is buried in the heavy rough and the identifying mark cannot be readily seen. In such cases, the player may lift the ball, without penalty, in order to identify it.

In order to lift the ball without penalty, the proper procedure must be followed. Before lifting the ball, the player must tell an opponent or other competitor, mark the location of the ball, and allow that person to observe the identification procedure. Once identified, the ball must be replaced so that no advantage is gained by lifting and replacing the ball. Except to the extent needed to allow for identification, the ball may not be cleaned. Failure to comply with the proper procedure results in a one-stroke penalty.

Hole Sixteen

Pennsylvania:

Cobaugh v. Klick-Lewis, Inc.,
561 A.2d 1248 (Pa. 1989)

Hole-in-One
Contests

A s any golfer knows, the ultimate thrill in the game of golf is hitting a hole-in-one.[65] In June 2006, Fuzzy Zoeller hit an incredible hole-in-one during the Allianz Championship at the Glen Oaks Country Club, Des Moines, Iowa. The ball settled in the rough next to the green on the sixteenth hole for about ten seconds before making a beeline for the cup.

Many amateurs also dream of hitting the "perfect shot," one where the ball finds the bottom of the hole, which is only 4-1/4 inches in diameter, after only one stroke. Yet, hitting a hole-in-one is a rarity for most amateurs. Some years ago, the magazine *Golf Digest* estimated that an average golfer had only a 1 in 20,000 chance of acing a par-3 hole of standard difficulty. The U.S. Golf Register estimated hitting any hole-in-one at 1 in 33,000.

Hitting an ace and winning a court case to claim a new car as the prize for a hole-in-one contest that was officially over several days earlier fit within the Ripley's "believe it or not" category.

In late spring, Amos Cobaugh was playing in the East End Open Golf Tournament on the Fairview Golf Course in Cornwall,

---

65. His spectacular shot may be enjoyed at www.youtube.com/?v=A3SJ1wtAAnU.

Pennsylvania. When he arrived at the ninth teeing area he found a new Chevrolet Beretta tantalizingly positioned, together with signs which said:

> "HOLE-IN-ONE Wins this 1998 Chevrolet Beretta GT Courtesy of KLICK-LEWIS Buick Chevy Pontiac."

The offer seemed clear: a free car to anyone who made a hole-in-one.

To his delight, Amos hit the perfect shot, a hole-in-one. The court records do not reveal the details of the shot, but who cares? A hole-in-one is an impressive feat regardless of how the ball finds its way to the bottom of the cup. In any event, when Amos attempted to claim his prize, the matter became more complicated.

The sponsoring automobile dealer, Klick-Lewis, refused to give him the car. It claimed the prize was for a charity golf tournament, sponsored by the Hershey-Palmyra Sertoma Club, that was over two days earlier. In other words, he was two days late. The dealer apologized for inadvertently neglecting to remove the car and posted signs prior to hitting his hole-in-one. The dealer said "sorry," but it had no obligation to honor the expired promotional.

Amos was not satisfied with the explanation. It was time to call in the lawyers. He sued the dealer to compel delivery of the Chevrolet Beretta. The parties entered a stipulation regarding the facts and then moved for summary judgment. The trial court granted Amos's motion, and the dealer appealed. The appellate court held in favor of the determined golfer.

Unilateral Contracts

The court found that the dealer made an offer that was accepted by Amos. A unilateral contract came into existence when

Amos performed in accordance with the terms of the offer by hitting the hole-in-one. It relied on the traditional principle that the promoter of a prize-winning contest, by making public the conditions and rules of the contest, makes an offer. If, before the offer is withdrawn, another person acts upon the offer, the promoter is bound to perform the promise by paying up. By its advertising signs, the dealer offered to award the car as a prize to anyone who made a hole-in-one. When Amos hit his ace he accepted the offer, thus forming a binding unilateral contract.

In order to be enforceable a contract requires consideration, which confers a benefit on the promisor or causes a detriment to the promisee. The court rejected the dealer's argument that the contract failed for lack of consideration. By making the offer to award one of its cars as a prize, the dealer benefited from the publicity generated by the promotional advertising. This benefit, the court said, was the required consideration.

Having determined that a contract existed, the dealer argued that the doctrine of unilateral mistake should excuse the performance of the contract. This argument is an extremely difficult one to win, as the automobile dealer learned.

Several factors led the court to reject it. First, there was no basis for Amos to think that the offer applied only to the earlier Hershey-Palmyra Sertoma tournament. The signs announcing the availability of the prize did not include dates or other such limitations. Thus, the court found that Amos had formed a reasonable expectation based upon the apparent terms of the bargain proposed by the dealer. Second, the court found that any mistake was due to the dealer's failure to remove the signs after the charity tournament. When the mistake is unilateral, not mutual, and is due to the negligence of the party seeking to rescind, performance will not be excused.

The hard lesson learned by the dealer: clean up after yourself by taking down your hole-in-one signs after the tournament. It's also prudent to specify who is eligible to participate in a contest.

One judge, who presumably was not a golfer, dissented. He argued that under Pennsylvania law, a hole-in-one contest had all the elements of illegal gambling. There was payment of money (the entry fee paid to enter the tournament), a reward (the car), and the element of chance.[66] This being the case, he reasoned that because all wagering contracts are illegitimate transactions which the law declares void, the illegal contract should not be enforced. He would leave the parties where it found them: Amos with the satisfaction of hitting the hole-in-one, and the dealer with the car. How would you like to have this fun-loving judge direct your next golf tournament?

Inside the Rules, Rule 15-3: "Wrong ball"

As illustrated by *Cobaugh v. Klick-Lewis, Inc.*, mistakes happen. When a golfer mistakenly plays the wrong ball, the consequences are generally straightforward under Rule 15. In match play, the golfer loses the hole. In stroke play, the player incurs a two-stroke penalty, and must rectify the mistake by "playing the correct ball or by proceeding under the *Rules.*"[67]

In the most common case, which involves a player mistakenly hitting the ball of another golfer in the same group before finishing the hole, the player must replace the ball hit in error,

---

66. The author of the majority opinion, Judge Wieand, had this to say about the element chance:

"Even if this Court could legitimately consider the "facts" which the dissent introduces from a popular magazine, those statistics demonstrate that a professional golfer is generally twice as likely to shoot a hole-in-one as an amateur golfer. Under these circumstances, it cannot be said that skill is "almost an irrelevant factor.""

67. Rule 15-3.b.

and find and hit the correct ball. Some golfers go to extraordinary effort in marking their balls in order to avoid the problem. Professional golfer Duffy Waldorf, for example, comes to mind. Duffy's wife and children mark his ball with messages and reminders. As a result, his golf ball is next to impossible to mistake.

The governing rule is that a player must play the same ball from the teeing ground until the player finishes the hole, unless a specific exception exists. The term "wrong ball" includes a ball belonging to another player, an abandoned ball, and the original ball when it is no longer in play.[68]

Some recreational golfers, especially when they have to hit over a hazard or risk losing a "favorite" ball, change balls during a hole. Other golfers may tee off with one ball and replace it with a different "putting ball" once they are safely on the putting green. These changes are no-nos. Even when the change is inadvertent, the Rules provide no exception to such wrong-ball substitutions.

As one might suspect, playing the wrong ball is not the best way to make new friends. It is also not a good idea to pick up a "lost ball" while it's still rolling.

---

68. Definition, "Wrong Ball."

Hole Seventeen

Federal:

U. S. Golf Association v. St. Andrews Systems, Data-Max, Inc., 749 F.2d 1028 (3rd Cir. 1984)

The U.S.G.A. Handicap Index Formula as a Property Interest

Golf courses are designed so that a proficient golfer can play eighteen holes in a "regulation" number of strokes. For most golf courses, the number of regulation strokes is between 70 to 72, and is referred to as the "par" for the course. Golf professionals and "scratch" golfers often score lower than par, whereas most amateurs usually score higher than par. As amateur golfers accumulate scores after playing each round, the scores are averaged and the difference between the average of the scores and par is conventionally called a player's handicap or index.

In the early 1890s a raging disagreement between St. Andrew's Shinnecock Hills Golf Club in New York and the Newport Golf Club in Rhode Island arose over which club's tournament conferred the title of national amateur champion. Out of this dispute, the United States Golf Association (U.S.G.A.) was created in 1894 to conduct national championships, to administer and promote golf, and to oversee the codification and interpretation of the Rules of Golf, as well as the Rules of Amateur Status.

Among the various services that the U.S.G.A. provides to an amateur golfer is a "handicap index." The index, commonly referred to by players simply as their handicap, has a simple objective. It allows golfers of different skill levels to compete with each other on an equal basis. The U.S.G.A. handicap system takes into account the difficulty of the golf course where a round is played and the golfer's past recorded scores. It also provides certain "safeguards" against the inflation of handicaps (referred to by golfers as "sandbagging") by excluding particularly bad holes and by counting only the "best" ten of a golfer's last twenty rounds.

The first version of the U.S.G.A. handicap formula was published in the late 1890s. A system based on a golfer's best three scores, devised in 1904, was adopted by the U.S.G.A. in 1911. Over the years, the formula has been modified to include a "course rating system" and "net score" (a score adjusted for course difficulty) method of handicapping; a "current ability" approach, in which only a golfer's most recent scores are counted; a system of "equitable stroke control" which disallows very high scores for individual holes; an upper limit on handicaps; and a "discounting" approach, in which a handicap is calculated based on a percentage (currently 96%) of the differentials between the player's score and the course difficulty.

A single, nationwide system was prescribed by the U.S.G.A. in 1958, and today more than 4.5 million golfers have U.S.G.A. handicap indexes. Most golfers know that this has not stopped the practice of "sandbagging." Some sandbaggers seem to have two handicaps: a lower one for bragging and a higher one for betting.

The U.S.G.A. litigated its exclusive right to this system. It sued Data-Max, Inc., to prevent the company from using and advertising the U.S.G.A. mathematical handicapping formula in the company's computerized handicap system. Data-Max was incorporated to provide golfers, primarily those players who did not belong to U.S.G.A. member clubs, with "instant handicaps." It used a computer program to calculate a handicap using the U.S.G.A. formula. Although Data-Max sold or leased its computer program to U.S.G.A. member golf clubs, it also marketed a subscription telephone handicap service, allowing a golfer to call in a new score and immediately receive an updated handicap, and to use its computer system to allow a golfer to directly enter a new score and receive an immediate updated handicap.

The U.S.G.A. advanced two legal theories to support its legal claim. The first theory was "misappropriation." The U.S.G.A. argued that it invested time, effort, and money in the creation of the formula, and that the Association was entitled to protection against Data-Max's wrongful use of their formula. The second theory was based on federal law, more specifically the false designation of origin provision of Section 43(a) of the Lanham Act. The U.S.G.A. asserted that Data-Max's use of the handicap formula violated federal law by misleading the golfing public into thinking that the U.S.G.A. had endorsed Data-Max's products and services.

The federal district court ruled in favor of Data-Max and the U.S.G.A. appealed. The U.S. Court of Appeals, Third Circuit, rejected the U.S.G.A.'s claims and ruled in favor of Data-Max.

State law and misappropriation

State law, not federal law, defines the boundaries of property protection available under a claim of misappropriation. Misappropriation is based on common-law principles that exist outside the statutory protections available under federal trademark, patent or copyright law. The theory typically has been

applied when a court finds that one competitor has dealt unfairly with another. In essence, "reaping where one has not sown."

The appellate court rejected the Association's argument of illegal misappropriation of its formula under New Jersey law. The court balanced the rights of the creator to exploit the ideas or information for commercial gain against the public's free access to the ideas or information.

The court also found that the U.S.G.A. and Data-Max were not directly competing in the same market. The U.S.G.A. was not in the business of selling handicaps to golfers. Rather, it was primarily interested in the promotion of the sport, and in its position as the governing body of amateur golf. The handicap formula was developed by the Association to further these objectives. Moreover, the U.S.G.A. was not directly affected by the number of official handicaps calculated each year or by the number of golfers who obtain handicaps.

In contrast, Data-Max was in the business of selling an "instant handicap" service to golfers who could not obtain "instant handicaps" through their clubs. They were "indirect" competitors. The U.S.G.A. did not object to the sale or lease of Data-Max's computers nor did it attempt to provide the direct services that Data-Max provides to golfers. Thus, it did not appear to the court that Data-Max's business would interfere with the U.S.G.A.'s incentive to maintain or update the handicap formula.

The interest of the public also loomed large. Acceptance of the U.S.G.A.'s handicap formula stems from the golfing public's desire to have a uniform system of quantifying recent performances in a way that allows equitable competition among golfers of differing abilities. The Association's system is widely accepted by the public. To require Data-Max to use a different formula, in the court's view, would effectively undercut its ability to provide a uniform handicapping service. Consequently, the public's interest in free access to this formula outweighed the competing interest in providing an additional incentive to the U.S.G.A.

On the facts presented, the federal court concluded that New Jersey law would require the U.S.G.A. to establish that Data-Max was in "direct" competition with it in order to succeed on the theory of misrepresentation, which it failed to do. Thus, the U.S.G.A. lost its misappropriation claim.

Federal law and false designation of origin

The federal Lanham Act governs trademarks. It protects those words, symbols, phrases, or designs that the public associates with a single source of goods or services. Section 43(a) provides the holder with a remedy against false representations that cause confusion or deceive as to origin, sponsorship, or approval. This section has been used commonly in advertising cases involving unprivileged imitation of a product or service.

The dichotomy between "functional" and "non-functional" is at the core of determining the merits of a false designation of origin claim. On the one hand, the functional aspects of a product or service are not protected by either a false designation of origin claim or a claim of trademark infringement. Functional features are not legally protected because their usefulness in identifying the source of the product or service is outweighed by the social interest in promoting competition and improvement, which are advanced by giving competitors free access to those features. The key policy served by barring the use of functional features from protection is the policy favoring competition. On the other hand, the use of "non-functional" features of a product or service to identify its source is legally protected against imitation by competitors, because the value of such features in identifying the source of the goods or services outweighs the social interest in allowing competitors to copy them.

The court found that the U.S.G.A. formula was functional. It was a simple mathematical method to derive a handicap from a golfer's posted scores. The U.S.G.A. formula was akin to an "industry standard." It allows the handicaps to be compared with one another, much as the standard gauge of railroad track allows a locomotive of one company to run on the track of another.

Industry standards are essential. Allowing one provider to obtain exclusive rights in such a standard would enable it to exclude competitors desiring to provide the same product or service, particularly if the original provider, such as the U.S.G.A. in this case, started with a virtual monopoly. The danger was evident to the court. To allow a monopoly over such a standard would defeat the policy of fostering competition that underlies the functionality doctrine. Being considered functional because there were no comparable alternatives, the U.S.G.A. formula was not entitled to protection under the Lanham Act.

The Legal Pendulum Swings

In *U.S. Golf Ass'n v. Arroyo Software Corp.*, defendant Arroyo developed a computer software program that used the golf handicap system created by the U.S.G.A. without its permission.[69] It also used the U.S.G.A.'s name and service marks to promote the software program. The U.S.G.A. asked Arroyo to stop using the handicap system and service marks, but Arroyo refused.

The U.S.G.A. sued in state court claiming misappropriation, unfair competition, and false and misleading advertising. The California trial court issued an injunction against Arroyo, based on misappropriation, unfair competition, and service mark infringement, and ordered Arroyo to stop using the U.S.G.A.'s handicap system and service marks. It rejected Arroyo's argument that the misappropriation claim was preempted by federal copyright law. Arroyo appealed.

The court of appeal affirmed the trial court's holding that the misappropriation claim was not preempted by federal copyright law. It held that the handicap system was not copyrightable under the Copyright Act and that the Act did not preempt a state claim outside the subject matter of the Act. Therefore, the misappropriation claim under state law was not preempted. The *Arroyo* case cited four unpublished cases supporting its position.[70]

The court declined to give conclusive effect to the prior

---

69. *U.S. Golf Ass'n v. Arroyo Software Corp.*, 69 Cal.App.4th 607 (1999).

70. The four decisions are: *U.S. Golf Association v. Data-Max, Inc.*, No. 89-CH-04995 (Ill. Cir. Ct., July 21, 1989); *U.S. Golf Association v. International Golfers Club, Inc.*, No. 103076-2 (Tenn. Ch. Ct., Aug. 1, 1994); *International Golfers Club, Inc. v. U.S. Golf Association*, No. 93-3246 (U.S. Dist. Ct., D.N.J., July 22, 1994); *Parsons Technology, Inc. v. U.S. Golf Association*, No. C93-318 (U.S .Dist. Ct., N.D.Iowa, Mar. 6, 1995). As a general matter, it is now recognized that computer programs are entitled to intellectual property protection, if they are not merely mathematical formulas.

findings by the Federal Third Circuit relating to claims of misappropriation of service marks regarding usage of golf-related systems because the record contained substantial evidence that U.S.G.A. had completely changed its handicap system by abandoning its older formula and developing entirely new formulas. In 1987, the U.S.G.A. adopted a "new" formula, including the "slope" system that measures the relative difficulty of a course for "bogey" golfers. A slope rating for a golf course can range from 55 to 155, with 113 being considered a course of average difficulty.

These more recent cases suggest that only a golf club or authorized golf association that issues and maintains U.S.G.A. handicap indexes in full accordance with the U.S.G.A. handicap system may use the terms "U.S.G.A. handicap index," "handicap index," "slope", and "U.S.G.A. handicap" without risking the wrath of the U.S.G.A. and a visit to the courthouse.

Inside the Rules, Rule 24: "Obstructions"

In *U.S. Golf Association v. St. Andrews Systems, Data-Max*, the U.S.G.A. claimed that the defendant "obstructed" its rights. The Rules of Golf also deal with obstructions. The guiding principle underlying Rule 24 is that relief from an obstruction should be available because it creates an unfair interference.

An "obstruction" is broadly defined to include anything artificial. It includes such things as cart paths, sprinkler heads, irrigation control boxes, bunker rakes, and discarded beer cans. Excluded from the definition, however, are objects defining the portion of the course considered "out of bounds," such as fences, walls, and stakes.

If the obstruction is "moveable," the rule is simple. The obstruction may be moved. If the ball moves as a result, the ball is simply replaced with no penalty.[71]

If the obstruction is "immovable," the situation is more complicated. Relief is available so long as the immovable obstruction interferes with the players swing or stance. In such a case, the player establishes the nearest point, no closer to the hole, where no interference occurs, and drops within one club-length of that point.[72] In order to avoid administrative difficulties, relief from the immovable obstruction is not generally available when the obstruction interferes with the intended flight of the ball. It would be too difficult to administer a rule based on the proposed flight path of the ball. But there is one exception where the "unfairness" is clear, however, and can be remedied without controversy. If the player's ball and the immovable obstruction are on the putting green, such as a sprinkler head, and it would interfere with the line of the putt, relief is available.

Golf fans will remember *"Tiger Woods vs. One Famous Boulder"* during the 1999 Phoenix Open. On the thirteenth hole, Tiger's drive put him behind a boulder which prevented him from having a rip at the par-five green with his second shot. PGA officials, cognizant of the loose impediment rule (Rule 23), concluded that twelve of the assembled spectators could assist in pushing the "loose impediment" aside because the boulder was not solidly imbedded.[73] The rest of the story is that Tiger went for the green, and made a birdie; he finished in third place.

---

71. Rule 24-1.
72. Rule 24-2.b.
73. Decisions 23-1/2, 23-1/3.

Hole Eighteen

California:

City of Santa Barbara Against the Use of Potable Water by the Tsukamoto Sogyo Company, Department of Water Resources Control Board, Decision 1625, February 15, 1990[74]

In Order to Conserve Water
RECYCLED WATER IN USE

DO NOT DRINK

NO TOME EL AGUA

Required Use of Reclaimed Water on Golf Courses

I n the United States, the demand for clean, reliable water is increasing. In the western states, effectively dealing with and managing water supply is a permanent part of the public debate. Mark Twain captured the importance of water in the West when he said, "Whiskey is for drinking, and water is for fighting about." This case is about a fight over water.

Golf courses compete with other users for access to scarce water supplies. Golf courses use water for many purposes, including general irrigation of fairways and greens, the maintenance of riparian habitat, and in lateral hazards and water hazards. The golf industry has known for some time that the availability of usable, unpolluted water is essential to the viable operation of golf courses.

Responsibly managing water supplies has led to an increased interest in the use of reclaimed or recycled wastewater for purposes other than drinking. The first national symposium on the use of recycled water for golf course irrigation was held in the late 1970s, and its symposium proceedings have become

---

74. Available at http://www.waterrights.ca.gov/hearings/decisions/wrd1625.pdf.

an important reference work on this topic. Since then there has been a continuing interest in golf and the environment, and not without justification.[75] The United States Golf Association, for example, believes that no issue is more likely to have a significant impact on the game of golf in the 21st century than how golf courses and golf maintenance affect the environment.

The City of Santa Barbara supplies potable water to users within its service area. It also collects and treats municipal wastewater at a city facility which it then sells to customers for additional beneficial uses unrelated to human consumption. Montecito Country Club[76] is within the city's water service area and buys water from the city. It operates an eighteen-hole golf course consisting of about 105 irrigated acres, a clubhouse, swimming pool, restaurant and tennis courts. The Country Club used potable water for golf course irrigation as well as for other uses. Faced with water shortages, the city proposed substituting reclaimed water for the potable drinking water used by the Country Club for irrigation.[77] The Country Club refused.

---

75. In 1992, the Environmental Protection Agency (EPA) published Guidelines for Water Reuse, the U.S.G.A. released *Golf Course Management and Construction: Environmental Issues*, and the American Society of Golf Course Architects published *An Environmental Approach to Golf Course Development*. In 1993, the U.S.G.A. sponsored a symposium on wastewater reuse, and published the symposium's proceeding in *Wastewater Reuse for Golf Course Irrigation* the following year. The year 1994 also saw the U.S.G.A. publish the *Landscape Restoration Handbook*, and the publication of scientific research on turfgrass in the *Journal of Environmental Quality*. The Center for Resource Management, *Golf Digest Magazine*, the National Wildlife Federation and the Pebble Beach Resort Company held the First Conference on Golf and the Environment. The involvement of the U.S.G.A. is documented at www.usga.org/green/index/html.

76. In 2004, the Montecito Country Club was sold by Tsukamoto Sogyo Company, Ltd. to Ty Warner Hotels and Resorts. The new owner reached agreement with Jack Nicklaus in 2005 to redesign the course.

77. California Water Code Section 13050(n) defines "recycled water," also called "reclaimed water," as "water which, as a result of treatment of waste, is suitable for a direct beneficial use or a controlled use that would not otherwise occur and is therefore considered a valuable resource." The Water Code contains numerous provisions controlling water reclamation and reuse.

Santa Barbara filed a complaint with the State Water Resources Control Board, which has jurisdiction over water and wastewater issues. The city asked the Board to require the Country Club to use its reclaimed water for irrigation purposes so that potable water could be freed up for other uses within the city. This possible water substitution was particularly important at the time because Southern California was in the midst of one of its recurring droughts.

To satisfy demand, Santa Barbara was augmenting its water supply through ground water pumping. This augmentation strategy was not a permanent solution because the ground water basins available to the city were already being used to capacity. Any long-term increase in ground water extraction could destroy the ground water aquifers due to seawater intrusion.

The Country Club declined to enter into a contract with the city for the use of reclaimed water. It had two principal objections. First, it was concerned that the salinity level or other pollutants in the reclaimed water might have an adverse effect on golf course plant life, particularly the greens. Second, it wanted some assurances. The Club wanted the city to hold it harmless for any claims that might arise from the use of the reclaimed water.

The California Law of Water Reclamation

The California legislature has declared the public policy for water reclamation in the state. Its policy is to encourage the development of water reclamation facilities as a way of meeting the public's growing water requirements. As an adjunct to this policy, the legislature has also prohibited the use of potable (drinking) water to irrigate golf courses if suitable reclaimed

water is available as determined by the State Water Resources Control Board.[78]

The Water Board, after giving notice and a hearing to an affected party, can find that the reclaimed water supply is of adequate quality and is available at a reasonable cost. If the state Department of Health Services agrees that such use will not be detrimental to public health, the Board may direct that the potable water use be stopped to allow the use of reclaimed water.

In the Santa Barbara dispute, the Board made the necessary findings required by Water Code Section 13550. It found that (a) reclaimed water of adequate quantity and quality is available for use at the Country Club; (b) the cost of the reclaimed water

---

78. California Water Code Section 13550 states:

"The Legislature hereby finds and declares that the use of potable domestic water for the irrigation of greenbelt areas, including, but not limited to, cemeteries, *golf courses*, parks, and highway landscaped areas, is a waste or an unreasonable use of such water within the meaning of Section 2 of Article X of the California Constitution when reclaimed water which the State Board, after notice and hearing, finds" adequate to meet state guidelines [emphasis added].

to the Country Club is comparable to or less than the cost of potable water; (c) the use of reclaimed water will not be detrimental to public health; (d) the use of reclaimed water will not adversely affect downstream water rights or degrade water quality; and (e) with the possible exception of the greens, the use of reclaimed water will not be injurious to plant life on the golf course.

But there was some uncertainty as to the effect reclaimed water might have on the Club's greens. Given this uncertainty, the Board ordered the club to designate one green that the city could use to conduct a test to determine whether the reclaimed water would be injurious to the greens. The test was to be conducted over a twenty-four month period.

The Board ordered the Country Club to stop using potable water for irrigation purposes as soon as it was reasonably possible to begin using reclaimed water. The city also was ordered to cease supplying potable water to the Country Club once the system for distributing reclaimed water to the Country Club was available.

The Board rejected the Country Club's demand that it be held harmless in the event damage occurred, although it did observe that the city's reclaimed water service contract provided some, but not all, of the assurances sought by it. In denying the request that the city hold it harmless, the Board reasoned that the law contained in the Water Code did not expressly require a supplier of reclaimed water to give indemnification assurances to users. In addition, the Board found that no evidence supported the conclusion that the cost of using reclaimed water was greater than the cost of using potable water. Finally, the Club presented no evidence demonstrating that the risk of litigation would be greater if reclaimed water were used instead of potable water.

What were the reclaimed-water test results to the green? Unfortunately, the results are no where to be found. Today the golf course uses potable water on all its greens.[79] This fact may suggest the Water Board was convinced that there was some legitimate concern with its use.

Today, reclaimed water is used extensively by golf courses in California, as well as in other states, for irrigation purposes and in water hazards. Although extensively regulated and monitored under state regulations, the question of liability for injury arising out of its use has not been litigated in the courts. One can predict with confidence, however, that it will be in the future. Whatever you do, the next time you are tempted to sponge off or drink from a water hazard using reclaimed water, resist the urge.

Inside the Rules, Rule 26: "Water Hazards"

City of Santa Barbara deals with the use of "reclaimed" or "recycled" water for irrigation on a California golf course. In addition to irrigation, reclaimed water may be used in golf course water hazards. Golf balls can perform amazing disappearing acts when water is involved. Rule 26 covers the situation when a player hits a ball into a water hazard, including a lateral water hazard.

The color of the stakes or lines used to mark the hazard is significant. Yellow stakes or lines are used to mark a water hazard, whereas red is used to delineate a lateral water hazard. The reason it makes a difference is that the options available to a player are different depending on the type of hazard.

---

79. In March 2007, a golf course representative, Bill Herbert, reported during a telephone interview with the author that the course uses potable water on all its greens.

A player has three options when a ball is hit into a water hazard, such as a pond or lake. A player may simply play the ball as it lies from within the water hazard under no penalty, apart from getting wet as a result of splashing around. Whether this option is available as a practical matter is going to depend on the actual facts. The second option is to play another ball from the spot from which the original ball was hit under a penalty of "stroke-and-distance." In the film classic *Tin Cup*, Roy "Tin Cup" McAvoy, played by the actor Kevin Costner, used this option when he repeatedly hit his ball into the water hazard. The final option, under a penalty of one stroke, is that the player may drop another ball anywhere "behind" the water hazard along an imaginary line drawn from the hole to the point where the ball last crossed the margin of the hazard.

Two additional options are available when the ball is hit into a lateral water hazard A ball may be dropped outside the lateral water hazard (not nearer the hole) within two club-lengths of 1) the point where the ball last crossed the margin of the hazard, or 2) at "a point on the opposite margin of the water hazard equidistant from the hole." A player, for example, would have the option of dropping on either side of a stream or drainage ditch marked as a lateral water hazard that runs parallel to the fairway. A one-stroke penalty is assessed for dropping a ball from a lateral water hazard.

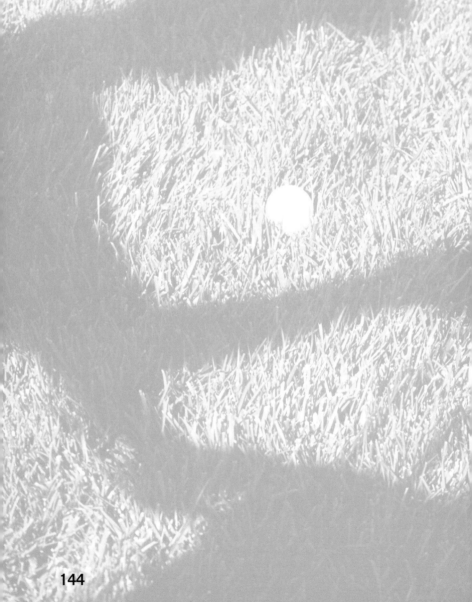

Hole Nineteen

Iowa:

Dolan v. State Farm Fire & Casualty,
573 N.W.2d 254 (Iowa 1998)

19th Hole
Drunken Assault

Many golfers enjoy the tradition associated with the nineteenth hole. This tradition usually involves a trip to the clubhouse bar, or something serving its reasonable approximation, where the order of business is apt to include "settling up" wagers won and lost, some laughs or "what-ifs," and a few drinks. On occasion, some golfers get carried away at the nineteenth hole, sometimes in handcuffs.

Walter Olson had finished at least twelve beers at the nineteenth hole when he realized that his golf clubs were missing. As you might suspect, he was at the time of this startling realization, to put it politely, intoxicated. Walter confronted Edward Dolan, an employee who was working at the pro shop, about his missing clubs. When Edward failed to produce the clubs on demand, Walter became physically aggressive. He was mad as hell and wasn't going to lose the missing clubs without a fight. He grabbed Edward's coat and pulled it over his head. In the resulting scuffle, Edward was injured.

The missing clubs were finally found. Walter had forgotten that he put them in his car before proceeding to the nineteenth hole. Mental lapses tend to occur after a couple of six-packs. While fortunate to rediscover the location of the missing clubs,

Walter was not so fortunate as to avoid the civil law suit brought by Edward and the criminal assault charges brought by the state of Iowa.

Edward sued the fractious Walter for negligence about a month after the incident. In November 1993, a jury agreed that Walter was negligent and awarded Edward almost $70,000 in damages. Walter was defended by an attorney provided by his homeowner's insurer, State Farm Fire & Casualty Co. Although State Farm hired an attorney to defend him, it reserved the right to contest the policy's coverage. The State Farm attorney was authorized to defend the personal injury claim against Walter, but the attorney had no authority to make representations as to whether the policy actually covered Walter's aggressive conduct.

Shortly after he was sued for negligence, matters took a turn for the worse for Walter. The state commenced a criminal action against him for criminal assault. Several months after the criminal charges were filed, Walter was found guilty of assault following a jury trial. His life was becoming increasingly complicated.

Walter saw the handwriting on the wall. He filed a petition in bankruptcy October 1993 in order to discharge or avoid any liability to Edward. Less than a month later, the jury found Walter negligent and awarded Edward close to $70,000 in damages.

Edward did not drop the matter. He had a judgment against Walter. In March 1994, Edward filed a lawsuit against Walter's insurance company, State Farm, for the purpose of collecting his unsatisfied judgment. Walter's insurance policy provided that liability coverage and medical payments to others do not apply to: "[A]. Bodily injury or property damage: (1) which is either expected or intended by an insured … ." The problem for

Edward was that Walter's insurance policy did not cover intentional acts.

The trial court found State Farm had no responsibility to pay the judgment entered against Walter because the policy excluded coverage for intentional acts. The fact that the jury had found Walter negligent in the original civil action did not control whether the policy exclusion applied. The jury in the original action did not determine whether Walter's actions were intentional. Thus, the finding that Walter was negligent did not prevent State Farm from arguing his actions were intentional and excluded from coverage. The Iowa Court of Appeals affirmed, and Edward took his battle to the Iowa Supreme Court.

The Supreme Court of Iowa found that jury's finding of Walter's negligence in the civil action did not preclude a subsequent finding that his actions were intentional. Its reasoning is enlightening: "We are not inclined to create a situation where the more drunk an insured can prove himself to be, the more likely he will have insurance coverage." A person who voluntarily becomes intoxicated does not make his intentional acts unintentional for purpose of insurance coverage. Because Walter had no right to enforce a claim against State Farm, neither could Edward.

In the end, Walter suffered a criminal conviction, went into bankruptcy, and took a tour of the Iowa civil court system. Edward also lost. He was left with an unsatisfied judgment against Walter. The fallout from nineteenth hole was more than anyone bargained for. Perhaps the only winners were the lawyers. They were fully utilized.

The lesson seems simple: Don't get carried away at or from the 19th hole.

Inside the Rules, Section 1:
"Etiquette; behavior on the course"

Drunken behavior is likely to involve the police, and not the technical aspects of the Rules of Golf. While *Dolan v. State Farm Fire and Casualty* involves a drunken assault at the 19th hole, some golfers can't wait until then before getting into trouble with the law.

The etiquette guidelines to the game cover safety to others and preventing unnecessary damage to the golf course. A player should take care to avoid anyone who might be hit by a club or other loose impediments that might be moved by the stroke or swing. The traditional warning "fore" is shouted when there is a danger of hitting someone with a ball. While the exact etymology of the term is uncertain, a popular view traces the term "fore" to military operations. During the 17th and 18th century, the infantry advanced in formation while artillery batteries fired over their heads. When an artilleryman was about to fire, he would yell "beware before." This fore-warning allowed the infantrymen to drop and cover to avoid being hit. On the golf course, the warning has been shortened to "fore."

But yelling "fore" is not always an adequate warning of danger. In 2006, for example, Adam Thompson was charged with felony criminal vehicular operation for driving a golf cart under the "influence."[80] Thompson and Anthony Savage had been drinking heavily during their round of golf. The two golfers allegedly had been slaking their considerable thirst with ample quantities of beer from their personal cooler as well as taking advantage of the Mississippi Dunes Golf Links roving beverage service.

---

80. United Press International, "Man faces DWI for golf cart crash," June 10, 2006.

As bad luck would have it, there was a cart operation problem. Savage wound up pinned under the golf cart cut, bruised, and with an injured eye. The police were called, and Thompson was charged.

Thompson's lawyer argued that the club shared some responsibility for the accident because the cart-girl continued to serve the two golfers after they were visibly intoxicated, something the club disputed. In essence, the claim seemed to be that the golf course was quite clever in putting an attractive seductress with a cart full of booze within Thompson's reach.

You be the judge.

About the Author

 John "Jack" H. Minan is a Professor of Law at the University of San Diego and an avid golfer. He has been Associate Dean for Academic Affairs, Acting Dean of Summer Programs, and the Director of USD's International and Comparative Law Programs at Trinity College, Dublin, at Magdalen College, Oxford, and in Florence, Italy. He has authored or coauthored six books, four contributions to books, more than forty scholarly articles, and numerous published reports and proceedings.

Jack has a B.S. from the University of Louisville, a M.B.A. from the University of Kentucky, and a J.D. from the University of Oregon. He has completed post-graduate course work in Operations Analysis at American University. Jack has practiced admiralty law as a trial attorney with the U.S. Department of Justice, and has qualified as an expert witness on matters involving Land Use Planning and Real Property.

Jack served as a gubernatorial appointee to the California Regional Water Quality Control Board from 1999 to 2006, and served six consecutive one-year terms as its chairman. Professor Minan served on the Board of Governors of the Southern California Wetlands Recovery Project, an organization consisting of seventeen state and federal agencies. He has been on the Board of the San Diego River Conservancy, a state agency dedicated to the acquisition and management of public lands in the San Diego Region, and served as its vice-chairman. Jack is active with the American Bar Association. He has served two terms (2005-06; 2006-07) as the chairman of the Environmental Law Committee, State and Local Government Section, and has been active with the Section Environment, Energy, and Resources.

Index